D1484202

By the Same Author:

About the Author

J V Stevenson was born in London, educated locally at the Battersea Grammar School and afterwards at Jesus College, Cambridge. He has been writing ever since he can remember. His novels and plays reveal him as a contemporary observer and satirist of unique vision, dramatic verve and remarkable originality. This has led him to be placed by critics in the 'old and strong English tragi-comic tradition' identified by Edmund Wilson as 'unparalleled in the literature of any other country'.

TANGIER TWILIGHT

J V Stevenson

ATHENA PRESS
LONDON

TANGIER TWILIGHT
Copyright © J V Stevenson 2004

ISBN 1 84401 258 1

First Published 2004 by
ATHENA PRESS
Queen's House, 2 Holly Road
Twickenham TW1 4EG
United Kingdom

Printed for Athena Press

Visitors do not, of course, expect to find – and would probably be disgusted if they did – in Tangier the entertainments and amusements of an ordinary European watering-place – bands, theatres, promenades, cafés, etc. The chief charm of a winter residence at Tangier is, next to its delicious climate, the opportunity it gives of meeting the English and American colony. They are inclined perhaps to hold themselves rather aloof from ordinary visitors and tourists; so visitors would find it advisable to bring introductions.

Eustace A Reynolds-Ball, FRGS
Mediterranean Winter Resorts
1896

To John Satterthwaite, who provided the introductions

Part One

Tangier: Grand Hotel Villa de France

5 January 197–

Arrived in evening bustle, *cinq à sept* in full swing. All along the road from the airport aged Biblical figures straggling beside young ones in jeans. People waving wares at passing cars: blankets, pots and pans, chickens. (Hard sell version of Home Counties' 'Eggs – enquire within'.)

Hotel perfect: waiters in fezzes, door-boys in djellabas, official beggar at gates. We seem the only guests. Unpacking, heard sound of muezzin. Also brass band.

Dinner in spacious old dining room. Mimosa on table, lights flickering throughout. Asked for red wine, brought white.

After-dinner stroll through town. Pleasantly seedy. Festive lights everywhere. None lit up. Streets deserted. Celebrated Café de Paris closed. Atmosphere of curfew. (Like English provincial towns when the shops shut.)

Still, balmy night air. Absence of insects sole sign of winter. (The Bishop has been diligent on our behalf: already three invitations waiting.)

6 January

Dawn. A full hour earlier than in London. Cloudless sky. We have 'The View': to the left through palms (three types) and blossoming mimosa, the kasbah, and beyond it the Atlantic; to the right Spain and the Mediterranean (strictly the Strait of Gibraltar).

Our room is large and airy – furnished in that final late-Fifties flurry of lightness and elegance, all inlay and tapering legs, mathematical mirrors and lamps; once despised, now cherished for its last remnants of style.

Brief survey of yesterday:
Few friends round for champagne breakfast send-off. Followed by interview with bank manager. Usual avuncular talk about 'over-spending': 'I know we're all apt to do it, but you may perhaps be

more apt than most...' I agreed, saying the cost of living is so high now we might actually save money by coming to Morocco. He said that might well be the case. I said nothing, wondering how he could fail to see that but for this trip we'd be perfectly in credit. He released the travellers' cheques. This, after the warning against over-spending, was giving us rope, if not to hang ourselves, at least to make our position ropier. (And concentrate the mind enough to flee before he could change his.)

In the taxi to the airport, driver said he'd visited Tangier: 'Oh yes, the old kasbah, the old medina, oh yes.'

I was still hobbling a bit from spraining my ankle last Saturday, but nothing would have kept me off the plane. After all the gloom and doom at home, desperate for stimulation and change of scene.

Perfect conditions to leave in: raw, rainy grey day. Motley bunch of passengers: a few women and businessmen, otherwise young males, English and Moroccan, singly and in pairs. Most distinctive, a quartet of barrister types in pinstripes. Very pukka. All except us stayed on for Casablanca and Marrakesh.

Began descent in golden dusk, cloud breaking as Europe slid away and Africa – a deserted beach – loomed ahead. As Istanbul was just Asia, so this was just Africa. The little airport – set amidst palms and plants – more orderly than Istanbul. No trace of flak from recent attempt on life of Sultan.

Customs very thorough till boy meeting us passed them notes. (Unnecessary: we had only duty-free drink.) He came up to me and whispered in my ear: 'Morocco Bound?' *With you, anywhere!* I thought; then remembered that was the name of the travel firm.

7 January

As usual after first full day in a place, feel as if we've been here weeks.

Despite gammy foot, walked eight miles (by pedometer). Complete tour of town: medina, kasbah, market, European quarter. Surprisingly rustic. White walls lining hilly winding lanes. Reminiscent of 'rus in urbe' London. Approaching the hotel at the brow of Rue de Hollande, you expect a country landscape to appear. Instead you see the Gran Socco full of buses and taxis and people pouring into the medina.

Everywhere being up and downhill, 'The View' constantly changes. Particularly stunning in the twilight.

Fingers smell of jasmine and mothballs. The first flowering everywhere in profusion. The second, the musty odour of Moroccan banknotes, the reek of which seems to draw the *Pests*, as I've named the inevitable 'guides' who've beleaguered us all day, fluent in the insults of many languages. I love their naked insincerity. They are all smiles and cringing ingratiation – 'You want boy, girl, hashish, souvenir camel?' – till you shake them off, when they hurl abuse at your retreating back. To date these have ranged from a modest 'Va t'en!' through a 'Bullshit!' to a full-scale 'Fuck off!' (from a three-year-old in the kasbah). They think 'Fuck off' offends you because 'Imshi' is offensive to them. (But then there are still people who find 'Fuck off' offensive.)

The Café de Paris is livelier than its dowdy closed-up look made it seem that first evening. From its curved terrace on a corner of Place de France you see the six other corners of the square, which has a little hill at its centre. So you are looking through 180 degrees at the passing throng who move in and out of your vision, like an old 'circlarama' cinema screen, or an opera chorus exiting one side of the stage to reappear at the other. The same people naturally reappear and the costume suggests a stage crowd. Someone passes in a sack-like djellaba, hobbling with a stick, like an outrageous Covent Garden upstager scene-stealing with an elaborate limp. Pests pass all the time, of course, constantly on the move (proprietor's insistence, I suspect), reduced to eye movements to pedal their wares. They even take the sugar from your table. *peddle, unless they're on bikes.*

Exhausted by the sheer *perpetuum mobile* of it, we walked slowly back here, eyes tired as from a flickering old film.

(One of our letters is from Alec Waugh. Invites us round any evening 'for a gossip'. Also a lunch invitation from someone called Brigadier Hasta. Have no idea who he is. He is not on the Bishop's list.)

We were sitting in the garden, basking in the sunshine, when a white-haired woman approached in that stately, formidable way that fills you with dread. This turned out to be Mrs Spicer, writer of our third letter. In it, she said she would 'call to sort something out' – 'call' in the old sense.

I ordered coffee. She insisted on going indoors to drink it. 'This is cold for us.' She wore an overcoat and gloves. (Greg and I were in swim trunks.) 'I hope for your sakes this lovely weather lasts,' she continued, adding, 'but we desperately need the rain,' in a tone so slyly insincere that, however sympathetic you felt to the locals' needs over your own, you could not help thinking Mrs Spicer would derive less pleasure from their benefit than your misfortune.

Although immaculate of poise, having the steadiness of a liner in port, Mrs Spicer seemed ill at ease. Her eyes were constantly on the move, as if expecting assault at any minute. She spoke in a heightened, almost hysterical tone of complaint. In fifteen minutes she had provided the perfect expatriate cameo.

'…There's a terrible water shortage here. When they cut you off, you have to listen to the lavatory to know if it's back…

'…Go to Gibraltar? What, at £30 a time, with the hotel? Oh, the Marks & Sparks is good but we live off the land…

'…No car. Walk everywhere; which means, being old, don't get about much…

'…Had to go to Britain last year. Dreadful place now…'

Preparing to leave ('Must go – work to do'), she said: 'Tangier for a month might seem rather dull to you.'

'We've brought plenty of books,' Greg said.

'Good. Light, I hope.'

G: We packed all paperbacks.

Mrs Spicer: Yes, paperbacks are good light reading.

'You should go to Fez,' she said as we accompanied her to the gates of the hotel. 'It's a wonderful place. I went there once. They think you can see it in a day. You can't. Got to stay the night.'

We fixed a date for lunch, some way ahead ('We're rather booked up, I'm afraid'). Mrs Spicer apologised for writing it in her diary. 'I was well brought up, you see, and one of the things one was taught was that we shouldn't write down an invitation because it suggests it's not important enough to remember. But as one grows senile it's absolutely essential to write it down. Otherwise there's no lunch to *seem* unimportant. Quarter to one,' she concluded. 'We still keep English hours. Some people adhere to the Spanish ones. We have American friends who invite you for one, and you're lucky to get anything by 3.30. Once, someone was ill there before he'd had a bite to eat! As for Moroccans—' (she inhaled deeply) '—well: they're so unreliable one doesn't buy the food till they've actually turned up!'

With a sigh, she set off into the market throng as if striding down Reigate High Street.

Tonight is really warm. We had coffee on the terrace of the little Moorish tiled courtyard and watched the staff go off duty. Like actors leaving the stage door after the performance. They emerge from a kitchen entrance at the side, their white jackets, black ties and fezzes discarded for sweaters and jeans. A little later the two night porters arrive, strolling casually in step together, already in costume – dark blue tunics, fezzes, baggy Ottoman breeches – as if for a late-night cabaret.

Evenings here are pleasant – thanks to our precautions: i.e. port, brandy, cigars. And music. Brought some cassettes. Among them the two little sonatas of Beethoven's Opus 31 (overshadowed by 'The Tempest' that goes with them). Their quirky comedy seems made for this place. Both have an uneasy serenity that suits the atmosphere – calm but a bit uncanny – as we sit after dinner reading and writing, windows wide open to the balmy night air, palms rustling in the breeze, a sound both idle and slightly sinister, perhaps through association with storms.

The owners here – a Dutch couple called van der Meer – told us Matisse stayed at the hotel in 1912/13, returning to Paris only for spring and summer. He produced 'a Moroccan triptych'. There's some doubt as to when the hotel was built. The van der Meers, who should know, say 1871 – as the French Consulate. My *Mediterranean Winter Resorts* of 1896 refers to it as established 'for half a century almost'. (Other quotes: 'Wild boar are plentiful

– see *Pig-sticking in Morocco*, by Lady Egerton'; 'Patients suffering from mental derangement ought to avoid Tangier.')

Have adopted Moslem practice and give generously to official hotel beggar each time we pass. When in Rome…

11 January

First full experience of what *Mediterranean Winter Resorts* calls 'the social gaieties of the small but lively English colony'.

Brigadier Hasta arrived on time. ('He's very punctual – he was in the Buffs,' Mrs Spicer said when I asked her about him. Also said he was rather deaf, so I began speaking quite loudly. His hearing seemed perfectly normal. I suspect Mrs Spicer is a troublemaker.)

Hasta, the complete retired brigadier: seventy-fiveish, dapper, fit; curious pink eye his sole defect. Took us in his car the mile or so to his flat in Boulevard de Paris, driving mainly on the left. 'They've renamed it,' he told us wearily. 'Ben-something-or-other. Most annoying. It's all this Moroccanisation.'

Flat very comfortable: has 'The View'. Pictures of military men in plumed helmets; set of Surtees on the bookcase; brushes laid out on dressing table. A well-ordered life.

In the sitting room, a man and woman stood drinks in hand admiring 'The View'.

'No, over there, dear,' said the man, pointing across the Straits. 'In *Europe*.'

With his stiff grey hair and beak-like nose, he suggested a cross between Edward Heath and the latter-day Auden. Despite his age, the air of the undergraduate hung about him; large ring on left little finger, woollen scarf round neck. (Everyone here behaves as though the temperature were close to freezing: this may be genuine acclimatisation, but also I suspect a ploy to counter any 'sybarites in the sun' idea.)

The Brigadier introduced the man in a mumbled tone, as if presenting a celebrity too well known to need naming. I caught 'Tommy' but missed the rest. The woman was called Miss Stray. 'Not *dis*trait!' she said with what really was a drain-like laugh. The sound exactly fitted the drooping, dowager-in-decay face with its rouge-and-wash make-up, hooded eyes and strategically placed warts. An immaculate green turban framed these distinctive features like the cascading folds of curtains around a stage set. Her appearance, for all its old-world formality, was distinctly raffish, I was thinking, when the Brigadier – as if making some telepathic pun – said:

'Miss Stray is ex-WRAF.'

'Based in Aden,' said Miss Stray, picking up the cue. 'Twelve years less a week. Lived abroad since childhood. In Tangier first in '32, then '35; '52 briefly, resident since '57. Great fun then. Contraband – cigarettes and alcohol. Now it's arms and drugs. No fun at all now.' She smiled broadly, then broke again into the drain-like laugh. As it reached its final gurgle, she took a sip of her gin and tonic, a sip large enough to confirm the suspicion of an influence other than elocution in her way of speaking. Her voice had debbish remnants long since overtaken by the needs of a racier, no-holds-barred type of talk that called for greater fluidity. Clearly this liquid quality owed its success to an almost literal means of production.

'I'm seventy. I tell people I'm eighty. Then they say I look young. I've got fifteen hundred a year. When I came here in '57 you could live off three hundred – and entertain.' (I suddenly remembered Mrs Spicer mentioning her: 'Very hard up.')

'I really am falling to bits. Left breast removed in Gib. Convalesced in Sussex. England's a horrible place now. Have you been to Fez? I'm very fond of Fez. I went there once. Darling!' she called to the Brigadier, 'this gin is gorgeous. I'm so poor I have to drink the Spanish stuff.' More plumbing sounds as she took advantage of this chance to have the real thing.

While she spoke, Tommy stood looking out at 'The View'. He had probably heard what she said many times before. But then he had probably seen 'The View' many times before also.

'Launcelot, I really must go,' he said finally.

'Must you?' said the Brigadier in a pained voice. 'Are you *quite* sure you won't stay to lunch?'

'I really can't, thanks,' said Tommy languidly. 'I have so many things to do.' He gave a pinched smile and drew his scarf up as if preparing to face the elements (not a cloud in the sky). Of course, there was no question of his staying to lunch; he had not been invited. But he continued the ritual of impeccable manners by saying to us, 'I hope you may find your way to Nettlewood,' as if we had announced some expedition to locate it.

'You must go to Nettlewood,' the Brigadier said when Tommy had gone – like him without suggesting how that might be arranged. 'It's a magnificent house. On what we call "The Mountain". The Mountain is very lovely. I used to live there myself. But at my age, I wanted somewhere smaller. You didn't seem too keen on Tommy today,' he added to Miss Stray.

'I *haven't* been too keen on him,' she said, 'since he told the Spicers how amazed he was I was still alive. He's absolutely right, of course,' she went on, 'it *is* amazing. I expect to drop dead any time. But I'd hate to do it before a good drink or a meal!'

Over lunch, she told stories of the criminals she'd known: among them the train robbers. 'I don't mind anyone, but I'm against dope-peddling and cruelty.'

The Brigadier, playing immaculate host, spoke little. ('Wonderful weather you've got – rather on the fine side for January.') He confined himself to preventing second rehearsals of Miss Stray's stories. She did occasionally repeat herself. Roughly every three minutes. 'You'll have to get used to it,' she said at one point, when the Brigadier stopped something coming up a third time. 'It's all part of my general decay. I had a friend once who forgot her own name in a shop. She had to play for time – ordered gin, tea, coffee, anything that came to hand, charging it all to account while she tried to remember who she was. Bought half the stock before it came back to her!' The cistern flushed. The Brigadier gave her a refill. 'Oh, all right. If we're going to get blotto!'

The meal was impeccably served. At the end of each course, the Brigadier rang a little bell to indicate that the plates should be cleared. 'Saves the servants unnecessary journeys, and us being overlooked.' Only once did it misfire, when Miss Stray, in mid-anecdote, slowed down her eating so that her plate was not finished when the servant, genie-like, appeared. 'Quite all right. Plenty of time,' said the Brigadier reassuringly.

'Hasta is an unusual name,' I said, to bring him into the conversation.

'Latin for "spear",' said Miss Stray.

'Yes, it's Hanseatic,' the Brigadier said, but without elaborating. Thus prompted though, he began to reminisce. A nice story about a wartime plan to take Tangier and Spanish Morocco. Secrecy sworn but a friend of the Brigadier's reported back to London. Brigadier dressed down by Foreign Office man. Didn't he know the American President and the Prime Minister had guaranteed the neutrality of Spain and Spanish overseas territories? Of course, says the Brigadier, but Tangier and Spanish Morocco aren't Spanish overseas territories. One an international zone, other a protectorate; so everyone had the right to be there. Good idea to claim ours before the Germans did the same. (He still sees the friend who ratted on him. 'We have an annual get-together. Never fail.')

Also, a story about 'forty niggers from Chad' who deserted from the French Army during the war. 'We were asked to help find them. French said they'd shoot the lot. French would. Well, the forty Negroes came over to us. Fine men. We took them willingly. Most useful. French agreed reluctantly. Said if they came back to Chad they'd get shot.'

Then, changing the subject, he talked about polo and horse-racing in Gib. 'The racecourse was where the airport is now. And everyone hunted of course. The Calpe Hunt was superb. No border in those days, let alone a closed one. Just waved at the guard and rode straight into the cork woods of Spain. That was after the First War. I went straight into the Army from Sandhurst. 1917, you see. Didn't get a shot at the Varsity. Never regretted it. Mind you,' he added a minute or two later, 'wouldn't have said no to a couple of years up at Oxford.'

A silence ensued, as if in respect for the Brigadier's lost university life. During it, I wondered if it was at all significant that 'Hanseatic' was an anagram for 'nice Hasta'... but didn't pursue the point. Instead, looking for a break in the hiatus, which was beginning to assume the proportions of a lament for the Brigadier's entire career, I raised the topic of the theatre (I'd noticed prints of *The Beggar's Opera* in the sitting room).

The Brigadier was most enthusiastic. His face became quite animated, except for the dead pink eye. (But behind his strong spectacles even this stood out by contrast, seeming to fix you in its lost gaze, as it may once have fixed a target through the sights of a rifle.)

'As a young man, I was very stage struck,' he said. 'I suppose that's why the Army appealed to me. Everyone in costume, barking lines to each other. I once saw Beerboh Tree as Cardinal Wolsey.'

'We used to have a drama society here,' said Miss Stray.

'Yes,' said the Brigadier, 'they did *The Beggar's Opera* with young Moors. It was absolutely atrocious. They'd never heard such music before, poor things. The theatre's terrible whenever I go back to London,' he went on. 'I don't want any deep message. Just want to be amused. No good, though. Who's that awful woman who used to run the Royal Court? Very left-wing. Put on kitchen soap plays. Joan Something. Littlewit, was it?'

Outside, drumbeats and the sound of a bugle.

'Oh, it's not a festa, is it?' the Brigadier asked wearily.

'The lights are all up in the streets,' I said.

'Doesn't mean a thing. They leave 'em up the whole time. So many festas they can't be bothered taking 'em down in between. Don't work anyway. Too many power failures. It's very tin-pot here.'

'There's a drama festival coming up in Gib,' Miss Stray said; she seemed to have missed the change of subject.

'Drama is prominent in the Colony?' I asked.

'Oh yes,' said the Brigadier. 'Well, you've got the Navy, haven't you? And the battalion.'

'They're doing *Charlie's Aunt*,' said Miss Stray.

'We did *Charlie's Aunt* in Constantinople in 1920,' said the Brigadier.

'What on earth were you doing in Constantinople in 1920?' Miss Stray asked.

'I was attending an audience with the last Ottoman Sultan,' the Brigadier said shortly.

Greg, who had looked a bit bemused throughout all this, made a bid at polite conversation and praised the flowers on the table.

'I love flowers,' Miss Stray said. 'Chrysanths are my favourite. D'you remember Lady Wade?' she asked the Brigadier. 'Someone told her all her guests were pansies. Later she said to her husband, "So-and-so said all our guests were chrysanthemums. Whatever did he mean?"'

The drain overflowed.

Coffee was served and the Brigadier spoke of his recent trip to Rhodesia. 'There's a fine spirit there. The people have come through. They're not defeatist. The men are big. Close to seven foot, many of them.'

'It's all the beef,' Miss Stray said.

The Brigadier showed no sign of hearing this. 'Didn't care for South Africa,' he went on. 'All tall buildings, huge cars, everyone rich and brash. Besides,' he added, without obvious change of subject, 'I like to see a single animal wild rather than a herd of them in a reserve.'

'I don't like South Africa,' Miss Stray agreed. 'I like South India.'

'I was in South India two years ago,' said the Brigadier. 'Took a bet Mother Gandhi wouldn't get back. I was wrong. Well, she's rather a fine woman, I think, Mother Gandhi. An altogether engaging old party. Bit too inclined towards Moscow, of course, but then she knows it's in her interest...'

'The Hubert-Smythes don't like her,' said Miss Stray.

'Well, they wouldn't,' said the Brigadier. 'Have you met the Hubert-Smythes?' he asked us.

'You should,' said Miss Stray. 'She's very sweet. And he's a lovely man. Was American Consul in Casa. Only don't get him on politics,' she added.

'Very eccentric views,' said the Brigadier.

'Used to be in the CIA,' said Miss Stray.

'Made an awful mess-up in Cambodia,' the Brigadier observed. 'The Cambodians are the kindliest, gentlest people in the world,' he went on wistfully. 'Also the Laotians. Always walk single-file in the jungle. More convenient. So when you see them in towns, they do just the same. Lovely people.'

We were back in the sitting room by now and G was browsing the library, which had a good selection of books on Tangier and Morocco in general. 'Haven't enough room,' the Brigadier complained. 'So if I get something new or better, have to weed out something else to make space. Of course, these Surtees are my favourites,' he said, handing G a volume of *Mr Sponge's Sporting Tour*. G took it and, trying to show enthusiasm, upset his entire glass of port over me. Miss Stray's drain positively flooded at this and even the Brigadier raised a hand to conceal a jerking of features (though I noticed the pink eye fix first on Mr Sponge to check for damage). 'You won't catch cold, I hope,' he said pleasantly. They have a nice line in *schadenfreude* here.

But am less concerned about my ruined trousers than to see the Hubert-Smythes and hear these 'very eccentric views'. As he was in the CIA they can't be violently left-wing. But if they're right-wing and yet 'eccentric' to the Brigadier...? I long to meet him.

Going up close to the official beggar this evening, I was sure he wore make-up. He definitely had mascara over one 'blind' eye...

12 January

Another bizarre day. No end to the stimulation here. Nor the material. Can't cope with it now. Too late.

Few brief notes re the Pests:

According to *Mediterranean Winter Resorts*, 'the traveller must not be surprised if he meets with insults or even rough treatment from the throngs of repulsive beggars and sturdy vagabonds. A calm and impassive demeanour should invariably be preserved.'

So: began with the friendly interested ploy. But they see this as a virtual contract of employment: was reduced to paying off one with ten dirhams (the price for his body in one wishful-thinking guidebook) as compensation for summary dismissal (couldn't take any more about the whereabouts of Barbara Hutton's house and the like).

Switched to the polite but firm 'no' to all approaches. This prompts the supposedly ingenuous retort (accompanied by mock-hurt expression) 'Why you come to Morocco if you no want talk Moroccans?' The double-think behind this outdoes the most devious politician. Useless to remonstrate in traditional liberal fashion that you *do* want to talk to Moroccans, but not about boys, girls, hashish and souvenir camels – which it would be insulting to them just to visit their country for. No good. They're long since inured to insult, have worked out a price-scale by degree of it. Have no illusions either about Morocco as a place where anything but the most mercenary conditions of life prevail. See no reason why visitors should come for any purpose but ones that ensure swiftest transfer of those musty banknotes into their eager hands. As everyone says who comes here: they've lost the Muslim virtues and acquired only the Christian vices. (But they think the same of you in reverse.)

Still, have devised a 'no' which, for all its politeness and accompanying friendly pats (they respond to touch; it's being ignored that they can't bear) seems to convey, if not the will of Allah, at least the infidel Rock-of-Gibraltar version (and the Rock is close enough here to give the comparison meaning).

Dinner tonight not wildly thrilling.

13 January

So: our visit to the Waughs.

They live, like the Brigadier, in Boulevard de Paris. We knew from going to his flat that it's been renamed and the signs taken down in preparation. So when we reached Place Kowait, turned right – G reckoning 97 (the Waughs') would be beyond 146 (the Brigadier's), because they must have 'The View'. But the numbers on that side were all even and, after the Brigadier's block, the buildings petered out. A new one was going up on the other side, which suggested that end of the Boulevard was only just being extended.

Back towards Place Kowait, though, I noticed a block numbered 117. My theory was that the Boulevard must continue on the other side of the square with the odd numbers then descending towards 97.

We crossed the square, G still doubtful because of the view question. As so often, he was arguing from the emotional standpoint (the Waughs couldn't possibly live on the side without 'The View'); I, from the logical one (the streets must, even here, have some system of numbering).

We then did a fatal thing. We asked for directions. Always a disaster in southern countries. G argued that in this elegant residential area the people would be more 'reliable'. Stopped someone getting into a car (sure sign of 'reliability'). Man assured us Boulevard de Paris was only to the *right* of Place Kowait. So retraced our steps, but again brought to a halt by sheer absence of buildings. What now?

★

(A pause, as I write, for the lovely moment each day when the rising sun catches the tops of the palms, casting their shadows against the sudden sunlit wall of the hotel garden – like the opening image at the start of a film. This first glimmer of light appears in an orange glow behind the hills on the other side of the Bay, then spreads across the town till, half an hour or so after dawn, it falls on the medina to the west. In that half hour the sky changes from pink to mauve, then settles on blue as the orange ball finally appears above the Spanish mountains and itself goes through a kaleidoscope of colour before assuming its full daytime dazzle.)

★

Well – we drifted back in a bemused state to the Place Kowait, which was becoming the *'Return to GO'* in the miniature game of Monopoly we seemed to be playing. Above the square in the harsh neon street light loomed the structure of the giant mosque which is being erected. Until now, the Spanish cathedral has been the tallest building in Tangier; but the Kuwaiti ambassador, seeing it on the skyline as he approached the town, thought it was inappropriate in a Muslim country that this distinction should apply to a Christian place of worship. Kuwaiti money was therefore provided to build a mosque that would outstrip it. In recognition, the square, that till then recalled a Spanish archbishop, now honours the donating nation. But 'Plaza' has become 'Place' and the French spelling 'Kowait' adopted: French money is still important. 'They won't rename the Place de France,' they tell you here.

As we stood in the square (which is actually a circle) the absurdity of all this seemed to match the absurdity of our own position: defeated by a simple address.

A boy of about fourteen approached and asked, politely and with none of the usual gush, if we needed help. In sneakers and a long, rather unflattering check jacket, he had the gawky quality of American boys: not at all the typical tourist hustler. We said we were looking for number 97, Boulevard de Paris. 'Ah yes,' he said, and offered to show us. We followed him as he led us back the way we had come. This should of course have warned us. That it didn't was partly because of his reassuring appearance, and partly because we now deluded ourselves into believing we had been on the *Avenue* de Paris. That was our mistake! Yes, the *Boulevard* de Paris was somewhere else – hadn't we passed it yesterday near the Place de France? – to which the boy was now leading us.

We had entirely retraced our steps, having walked some ten minutes, when the boy stopped in the Rue de Fes and, pointing to the building on our left, said, slightly plaintively, 'Va bien au cinéma?'

All was suddenly clear. The boy had interpreted our enquiry as a sexual overture and was now suggesting we enter the cinema for the purpose. To his amazement, we went into howls of anguish and doing an about-turn set off in the opposite direction at a frantic pace. The psychological effect of this on the boy cannot be exaggerated: two Englishmen who did not want sex with him! Will he ever recover?

We returned to the hotel and phoned Alec Waugh. He seemed to find it inconceivable that we'd had so much trouble locating him: 'I'd say you can't miss it, except you have.' I suggested perhaps another evening as we were now so late. 'Oh no,' he replied. 'We've got food prepared.' (G at this thought we should tell the hotel we would not be eating but I demurred: I'm sensitive to the subtle distinction people of the Waugh generation make between 'food' and 'dinner'.)

Off we set again and within five minutes we were at the fatal point where G had asked the way. Two doors from there we now found number 97...

Waugh himself opened the door. A very small man – smaller

even than Evelyn and looking every bit like the Osbert Lancaster caricature of his brother, but with kindly, not fearsome eyes. Wearing a smoking jacket decorated with bright flowers and strawberries, of which Evelyn must deeply have disapproved. But Alec, a confirmed lover of women throughout his life, has no inhibition about sporting the kind of garment that would unnerve a man of less certain sexual taste.

He ushers us into a spacious, conventionally decorated room, dominated by the large figure of his wife. She wears a billowing blouse and high-waisted skirt of the kind you see in 17th century Dutch painting. Her grey-black hair is swept back into a bun that for some reason recalled the name Martha. She is actually called Virginia and is half-Danish, her forefathers having migrated from Jutland to Utah, where she had a Mormon upbringing.

A few garbled exchanges about our getting lost: 'Why 146?' Waugh asks. 'I can't see why you went to 146.' He has missed our reference to setting our sights by the Brigadier's address. Like his brother, he is very deaf, deafer of course at eighty than Evelyn was at sixty. *Tone* deaf like him, too; unable to abide music. (He said the Moroccans here did an 'excellent' production of *The Beggar's Opera*. Virginia: It was terrible, Alec! Waugh: It must've been if I enjoyed it.)

But our main problem is that, apart from being exhausted by our wanderings of the past hour, we sense a barrier between us, legacy of the 'Evelyn brigade' who descend vulture-like for stories 'of your famous brother'. It would be easier, of course, if we had come for that purpose: we would then take care to conceal it. But our anxiety to show we are without such motives only makes us appear all the more to have them. Similarly, Mrs Waugh, to dispel any idea that she sees our visit in that light, gives exactly the impression of vetting us with it in mind.

A situation of superb dramatic irony thus develops. The Waughs have invited us out of pure hospitality and we have come to see them entirely for their own sake. Yet we sit rattling the ice in our drinks and tentatively nibbling at our cocktail biscuits (G looks relieved that we didn't cancel dinner) as though taking part in an interrogation where a single word will give us away. Conversation is stilted and intermittent. The need to talk loudly for Alec Waugh to hear removes any subtlety or nuance it may have (reminding me how fatal to acting has been the habit in the West End of spelling things out for foreign audiences). Questions are asked and answers given. A certain time is allowed each topic and the acid test is brevity.

Does G know the doctor who treated Mrs Waugh in London?
No, G does not.
Am I a member of the PEN Club?
No, I am not.

An even when we go beyond this, I feel that, as in an exam, we are answering questions we've no interest in being asked, the kind that can only elicit boring replies. Before long, Mrs Waugh was leading us into the Panglossian abyss where everything was so *nice* and everyone so *charming*; wasn't life just *wonderful* and didn't the world seem a *fascinating* place?

The result is that Waugh himself hardly gets a chance to speak. We were seeing in miniature the futility of security systems: you soon reach the point where the object or person so protected is lost from view, and the security operation exists in its own right.

This was unfortunate since Waugh is a genial, delightful man. When he did speak, he was entertaining. I liked his rapid, old-style clipped delivery, its staccato speed losing nothing in the clarity of diction. When I asked him if he'd been to a particular place, he said – the words coming in machine-gun syllables – 'I-think-I-never-have-done-so.'

But by now, we had reached the level of desperation where the most harmless remark is open to misinterpretation. Mrs Waugh explained that she had first seen Alec in a picture in one of his books: 'After that, I was determined to see him.'

'You did much better than that,' I heard myself saying, without for a moment intending the implications.

'Would you please stand your drink on a mat?' Mrs Waugh asked G. 'I like to protect my table.'

'Of course,' came G's well-meant but crushing reply: 'Is it teak?'

I had meanwhile scrupulously avoided even a glance at the book *Evelyn Waugh and his World* which lay on that table before us. In our present state, it was not difficult to see it as a trap laid for the Evelyn brigade, the perfect cueing device for accounts of 'the famous brother'. But steering clear of the pitfall made me alight on our salvation. For my eyes had strayed instead to the book at the other end of the table: a Wisden Cricketers' Almanac. Perhaps this, in a version of Portia's caskets, was intended as a test for the visitor, Alec being – unlike his brother – a passionate cricket fan. Was this the victorious leaden casket, outwardly drab, the key to our host's heart? Would the literary equivalents of the Princes of Aragon and Morocco (appropriately in Tangier) come to nought lured by the glitter of the Evelyn trap?

I hesitated only because I knew that to raise the topic of cricket in this way would exclude G forthwith from the conversation. But at that moment, G, in a supreme act of self-sacrifice, raised it himself. He opened the Wisden casket.

Instantly all was transformed. Waugh was reminiscing about Stopford and the '48 Australians, the Timeless Test and the Bodyline series, and Mrs Waugh was relaxed, and silent; immune to the subject but aware that to Alec it was virtually the source of life itself. Within minutes Waugh was saying we must have lunch on Sunday. 'You'll probably need a change from the Villa de France cooking – never been awfully good.' And before lunch we'd have 'the best martinis in the world' at Porte's Salon de Thé. Virginia probably wouldn't come; they rather knocked her out. (Virginia: What? I'll come! I'll have a whiskey sour!) We would meet at the English Church after service. 'Gives you something to look forward to during the sermon.'

As we were leaving he showed us a small privately printed book about a J C Squires' cricket team. And early editions of his travel books, which we'd talked about with him. ('Evelyn and I divided the world up between us.') 'I'm so glad you've read *some* of my books,' he said. 'Specially the ones you have.'

(Four new arrivals here today. Exactly the same pukka types who came out on the plane with us.)

14 January

They *are* the four who came out on the plane with us! It was a bit grotesque to imagine a second pukka quartet. They have been in Marrakesh where they say they had less pestering in a week than they've had here today. One of them was kicked. They refused to give any dirhams and were told someone would wait outside the hotel *day and night* and cut their throats. They reported this to the police, but the police said it was unlikely because Moroccans become apathetic about everything after a time, even throat-cutting.

Am becoming addicted to the local French language newspaper, *Matin du Sahara*. Marvellously biased. Consists almost entirely of eulogies of the Sultan (as Moroccans – aware of his dynastic descent – call Hassan). *Matin* refers to him as 'Sa Majesté', S.M. for short. Desperate attempts to turn S.M. into a figure of international consequence: S.M. in London, S.M. in Paris, S.M. sending a communiqué to the US president, etc. Also numerous reports of 'gloire' and 'victoire' in the Polisario war. As usual in such cases the truth emerges by default: if there is all this to celebrate, why today, for instance, are we treated to a long paeon to S.M. for setting up a Royal Commission to further national development of 'le football'? (But: this evening on Gib TV, a nostalgic costume serial followed by something called *Jersey under the Jackboot*. Both programmes made in Britain. Which says as much about Britain as it does about Gib.)

15 January

An incoherent American keeps ringing up asking us to play bridge. Can't make out his name. Either Brandon Brendon or Brendon Brandon.

We went to the hill called the Charf for the view of Tangier (after lunch by the pool – which is much closer to Spain than the Spanish omelette we were given).
   Out past the Syrian mosque and the abandoned bull-ring, the

bus dropping us on the far side facing away from the city. A peasant straight out of Lawrence escorted us across patchy fields where mangy sheep grazed in desultory fashion (explaining the toughness of the hotel mutton). Up a stony steep path, hillside strewn with old women and children making their way 'home' – i.e. huts (not unlike British pre-fabs). All with views of light industry.

As we climbed, we saw a group of women washing baby clothes in a stream, using traditional scrubbing boards and singing as they worked. Nothing traditional about the baby clothes: genuine consumer article. An image of what is happening here.

Wandered through the village. Small-scale farming: chickens; odd cow by owner's dwelling; more mangy sheep. All around, happy little children. Girls dancing, boys playing football. Boys waved, girls said, 'Good evening' in Spanish. Relief to find signs of disinterested friendship after the Pests.

Came down fashionable side, view of city before us. Atmosphere quite different. Well-made road leading down from fir-treed summit where grandest villas command best positions. But entire road lined with beautiful villas, red-hot pokers and bougainvillea spilling over walls. Well-dressed schoolchildren making their way 'home' – i.e. said villas. Some ride on horseback. Suburban atmosphere prevails. No one greets us.

Back through a wasteland of rubble, desolate ground and unfinished building where the new town is being developed. According to the Waughs, it was Lord Bute's Minzah Hotel – put up after World War I – that dictated the siting of the modern town above rather than along the Bay. Certainly making up for it now.

This – the Tangier Beach – in great contrast to the Town Beach on the Atlantic side of the port. There, sewage (looking suspiciously untreated) spills out; wild dogs scavenge; on this (Mediterranean) side, all the resort facilities – closed now for 'winter', though today's warm sunshine would do justice to Brighton or Blackpool in July.

Walked back along palm-lined promenade. Shades of Nice but 'grand' hotels seedy. Outside the Rif, a tall, weather-beaten Pest in black suit said: 'You like fuck girls? Fuck boys? They fuck you? Same? I like fuck boys.' He seemed in a hurry. 'We go fuck, yes?

In shower, ship, beach, hotel? After, smoke kif, eat Moroccan food.' He showed us an old photo of himself. He looked very different. Another boy passed. 'Him too? Yes? All go, in shower, fuck, eat Moroccan food? Or eat Moroccan food, smoke kif, fuck after? Or smoke kif, fuck, eat Moroccan food?' The permutations seemed endless. 'Or no today – tomorrow: fuck, smoke kif, eat Moroccan food. Or *no* fuck, smoke kif, eat Moroccan food. Or just talk in café.' He spat on the ground. Said bitterly: 'Go from here!'

Another poor dinner. Alec Waugh is right about the food here. It is seldom bad, but never good. The menu itself a masterpiece of euphemism for what is impeccably put before you. A glance at the English translation prepares you for the worst. Tonight we had *Potage Apollo*, *Fricassé de Bœuf Monte Carlo*, and *Dessert Solferino*. This came out as:

> *Apollo Dish*
> *Thin Maitre d'Hotel Grilled*
> *House Tart*

(There is a nice old German barometer in the courtyard here. Why German? I always tap it on the way in and out. Tonight, it's falling. Shows 'veränderlich', which I think means 'changeable'.)

16 January

It does. An understatement tho' for today's cloud, rain and cold wind. August Bank Holiday weather. Arctic by the standards of here. All the British in furs.

Luckily, this coincided with our lunch at the Spicers.

We had spent the morning browsing in the excellent Librairie des Colonnes, which confounds Mrs Spicer's view that there are 'no books here'; there is a library at the British Consulate as well. I bought Jane Bowles' novel, *Two Ladies*, unavailable in England.

The shop is run by two *old* ladies. They told us that when Genet was in Tangier, he never had a bank account; always collected his royalties from the bookshop. This was convenient for him since it adjoins the Claridge Restaurant where he would sit on the terrace eyeing passing boys. Boy and money to pay him could therefore be picked up together. (In general, though, Genet's life here strikes me as unenviable. Have just read a book about his stay in Tangier, where he seemed like an ageing Joe Orton. Perhaps Orton was lucky to die young.)

From the bookshop it is a short walk along the Boulevard, down Rue de la Liberté and through the Gran Socco to the Spicers' house on the edge of the medina. Walking any distance here is like moving between two film sets: one for an Old Testament epic, the other for a Europe that seems more remote even than that. Cafés and shops circa 1948, old-style saloon cars gliding along the Boulevard, from where a big dipper of Time sweeps you down to the market and back to the Bible. On the way (in the Rue de la Liberté) the two film sets merge: extras from both productions take a break with pals from the lot next door ('Has Moses appeared yet? We're on Bogart and Bacall at the airport'). The casts of both films have a heavy male bias, but the female roles aren't exactly unremarkable. What you might call prominent non-speaking parts: i.e. gagged. (Intending housebreakers would do well to study the knots which look impregnable.) They go about in pairs muttering to one another and instinctively moving away at the sight of a camera. Dreadful mother-in-law jokes keep coming to mind: gags about women being gagged etc. Acting with the eyes isn't in it. No other feature is visible. The young, unmarried ones – free of all this – flaunt outrageously. The contrast makes you see how bare ankles once had the ability to shock in England.

The Spicers' house is magnificent – Moroccan in design with an inner courtyard and a gallery above. Ground-floor rooms around courtyard heavily barred: originally women's quarters. Now furnished in old English style, the place has a hybrid air, especially on a cold, grey day like this with the wood-smoke smell of the fire. You step in from the crowded Arab market, which grew up around the house, and find yourself in a Sussex cottage.

We were the last to arrive, having interpreted 'quarter to one' for 'one'. But timings here are most specific and everything is on the quarter: lunch, quarter to one; dinner, quarter to eight (but dinner is rarely given: people stay in after dark).

There were three women and five men. 'Our two visitors both being male, one can't have equal numbers,' Mrs Spicer apologised. (During lunch she referred to E M Forster as 'that dreadful old man'...) We sat in large winged armchairs drinking gin and tonic and eking out the conversation, aware that rationing was in order if we were to get through the meal. The atmosphere of the party suggested a pre-war lunch in provincial England. The other guests were: an ex-district nurse, a little squirrel of a woman, dull and pleasant, very knowledgeable on Morocco and fluent in both classical and colloquial Arabic; a healthy-looking sixty-year-old called Raymond, former businessman now writing a biography of W B Harris, *The Times'* man in Morocco at the turn of the century; a girl with a Liverpool accent, courier for some travel firm (whom Miss Stray mentioned at the Brigadier's: married to a Moroccan and invited always to make up the numbers; she was very deferential and wore a neat two-piece 'costume' for the occasion); and lastly, the vet, Cassell, who was a cross between Dickens' Mr Skimpole and the Mad Hatter: wild grey hair, swept across from low left parting; lean aged looks with youthful complexion; squeaky voice. I have always had a rather low opinion of Agatha Christie's characterisation. Now I realised I was wrong. Here was a group which could have been lifted from anywhere in her *œuvre*. My spirits rose.

The star of the occasion was Henry Spicer himself. A genuine old-fashioned crank of the first order, the collector's showpiece. Slim, grey-haired, grim-featured, tweed-suited, cheeks hollowed, with that odd square-legged British stance, slightly leaning forward when serving drinks but legs never bending, as if to do so would be effete. Very blimpish, very philistine ('A writer? Well, I know nothing at all about *that*'), absolutely predictable ('There's a very big difference between an air fare of £60 and one of two hundred, *isn't there?*'), a pasty seventy-year-old completely at odds with the world, a fascinating anachronism, the absolute stereotype of pre-war middle class man – the kind now depicted in advertisements for 'Gentlefolk in Distress'. I took to him at once.

Spicer though is not at all 'in Distress'. He is very well off. He plays the stock market and has just sold a plot of land on the Mountain to Raymond. 'Thought I'd hang on to it for when I'm too senile to climb these stairs and have to move into a flat, when it would make a nice garden. Can't afford it any more though.'

'It must be pleasanter keeping a garden here than in England,' I suggested.

'Oh God, no,' said Spicer. 'I much prefer an English garden. You know where you are with the seasons. When you see the crocuses coming up, you know spring's on the way. Here, something comes through, then it may be a month before other things do the same. I'd live in England any time – if I could afford to.'

He was at Brasenose in the Twenties. 'Many of my contemporaries have become famous. I never knew any of them. I rowed. Brasenose was hearty in those days. It's become intellectual now, I gather. I still watch the teams. They come from new schools now, many of them. Cambridge still seems to recruit from the old schools. I don't mind the newer places getting in. I went to a newer place myself. Still, good to see the *old* places figuring.'

As we sat down to lunch, Spicer explained his method of countering what he called 'the foreigners' ability to talk about you in their own lingo'. He spoke only English, so had recourse to a dialect he had himself devised and named after his native Herefordshire.

'You just take off the first letter and put it on the end, adding "a" or "we" depending on whether it ends in a consonant or a vowel. So: "plate",' he went on, taking one from a passing servant, 'becomes "latpa". "Glass"—' (he drew his own from the man who was filling it) '—is "lassga". "That man's a fool" becomes "Hatta ansma oolfa". Try it,' he urged.

We all tried it. When he saw we were having trouble, he resumed: 'You can elide things to make it smoother. I've even thought of Russifying it, adding "ov" or "ski" here and there just to confuse them.'

The irony of all this is that Spicer's jerky style of delivery makes him difficult to understand anyway. His instructions to the servants seemed as incomprehensible to them as they were to me. I wondered what language he could possibly be speaking: it sounded like no conceivable Arabic, French or Spanish, just a series of incoherent grunts accompanied by wild gestures of impatience and vague wavings of his arms toward various guests. It must have been that kind of pidgin English people think will get through if spoken in a loud voice.

These odd noises were accompanied by Mrs Spicer's imperious summons on a clanging table gong – much larger and louder than Brigadier Hasta's. (The house was full of ringing. The front door bell had a doom-laden sound and the clock chimed in imitation of Big Ben: 'It's bewildered by the climate,' Mrs Spicer explained.)

Somehow the servants understood all these commands. They must have been immaculately trained by the virago herself. They appeared punctiliously and served everyone in correct order: lady guests, male guests, hostess, host – the latter with some difficulty through the flailing arms and torrent of meaningless sounds.

The table talk was haphazard to say the least. A topic having been raised would be ignored or instantly suppressed by someone else. Most remarks were greeted with huge laughter from Mrs Spicer, whose idea of the perfect hostess meant finding anything anyone said excessively funny. The whole thing proceeded at breakneck speed so that even if you started a conversation with your neighbour an interruption soon put paid to it.

'I do love a circus,' someone – the district nurse, I think – said à propos of nothing.

'I don't,' said the vet. 'I know how they train the animals.'

Normally, that would have been that, except that on this occasion, Mr Spicer took up the theme: 'I like acrobats,' he said. 'It seems to me a waste of time for a man to spend his life teaching a seal how to change into second gear on a motorbike. I think it's more degrading for the humans than for the animals. Don't you agree?' he said to me, as if the writer among us were the one to judge so high-minded a question.

Before I could reply, someone asked how a 95-year-old woman called Mrs Févier was.

'Very poorly,' said the travel bureau girl. 'She's just been to London and back by bus.'

'By *bus*?' Spicer's arms flailed and his cutlery almost went to the wind.

'It's cheaper,' said Raymond.

'And you don't have to change,' said the district nurse. 'It makes sense really for an elderly person.'

'An alcoholic on board dropped dead,' said Raymond.

Mrs Spicer rocked with laughter. (I suddenly placed her in the Christie canon: she was Mrs Boyle from *The Mousetrap* who, to everyone's delight, is murdered at the end of Act One.)

But we had moved on.

'You know, the news is getting worse every day,' Spicer was saying.

'I've stopped listening,' said the nurse. 'I just get the weather from Gib.'

'It was 48 this morning,' the vet put in.

'I think today's news was the most depressing I've ever heard,' said Spicer.

(The Brigadier made the same remark at his lunch, and I said: 'Worse than 1940?' I said the same now. You pick up the local habits very quickly here.)

'*The Daily Telegraph* costs ten shillings,' said Mrs Spicer to Greg. 'And it's always days old. Except Thursday when for some reason it arrives in the evening. If you can be bothered to go out and get it.'

'I never go out after dark,' said the travel bureau girl.

'*The Daily Telegraph* is a fine newspaper,' said Mr Spicer.

'The Moroccan doctors are very good here,' the vet said to me.

'Don't say "Moroccan", say "Moorish",' said Raymond.

'*The Guardian* is a terrible newspaper,' said Mr Spicer.

'But though they've got the equipment, it's not in use,' the vet continued.

'There's no nurses to do the follow-up either,' the nurse observed.

'Whenever there's anything ridiculous quoted on the wireless, it's always, "Says *The Guardian*".'

'When he collapsed on New Year's Eve, no one even felt his pulse,' said Mrs Spicer, pointing at her husband.

'They thought he was drunk,' said Raymond.

'Moroccans drink plenty of alcohol themselves,' Mrs Spicer put in.

'Don't say "Moroccans", say "Moors",' said Raymond.

'They only drink the expensive stuff too,' Mrs Spicer went on.

'Well, you have the Chief of Police here,' said Raymond.

'It's useful to know someone like that,' said the nurse.

Meanwhile Mr Spicer had grown merry. He was with varying degrees of success recalling some rhymes of his youth.

"'My name is John tum-te-tum Jowitt

All that's knowledge is if I m'self know it

I'm the master of this college

And what I *don't* know isn't knowledge.'"

'Oh, give them the Curzon one!' his wife urged, doubled up with laughter.

"'My name is John Llewellyn Curzon

I am a very superior person

My something's something, my hair is sleek,

I something something something Greek.'"

'He's forgotten it!' Mrs Spicer spluttered out, in a helpless condition.

Soon afterwards, the ladies retired. 'We'll have a brandy while they go upstairs,' said Mr Spicer.

We five men sat ruminating on the world – or rather, Spicer did. Apart from his other quirks, he is an ardent Francophobe. (At lunch he'd insisted I say 'Marrakesh': 'Why say it the French way?')

Now he railed against French influence.

'If not Britain, then America,' he intoned. 'Rather than those damned French. We were conned by them in 1904 with the Anglo-French Entente. Gave up our influence in Morocco – which had *huge* potential – for control in Egypt – which hadn't any. Can't blame them. Only looking after themselves. *But why weren't we?*'

He spoke of the superiority of the white races. The vet tried to mediate. 'I think the best of them are as good as the best of us.'

Spicer started to agree, then checked himself:

'Oh no, I don't really think even that, you know,' he said genially.

Suddenly he launched into a diatribe against Christians.

'Many Christians are the real racists!' he averred. 'They don't like animals. What could be more racist than that? Animals are our fellow creatures. I sometime wonder if we ought really to kill them.'

The vet pointed out that the same could be said of vegetables.

'I suppose so,' from Spicer.

The vet: 'You kill millions of organisms anyway with every glass of water you drink.'

Spicer reflected on this. Concluded: 'Yes. It seems no life can exist without the destruction of other life.'

With this observation we went up to join the ladies.

Mrs Spicer was handing round cigarettes. 'You don't smoke of course, do you, doctor?' she said to Greg; and to me: 'You only go in for the grander things.' (She has a brilliant capacity for recalling the smallest detail for future use: on our first meeting I had expressed my preference for cigars.)

Raymond explained how he and Tommy *Bidfine* – as it turns out that Audenesque figure is called we met at the Brigadier's – smuggled whiskey in from Spanish Ceuta. They made a rubber sculpture of someone else in the Colony, an old man called Esmé something. This sculpture they would fill with whiskey, keeping it in a sitting position at the back of the car. At the frontier they showed the old man's passport but begged the Spanish customs not to disturb the 'poor old feller' who, as they could see, was sound asleep.

'Mr Raymond and Tommy Bidfine are the young blades here!' the ex-nurse told me.

'What does Mr Bidfine do?' I asked, anxious to know more about that intriguing, muffled-up person. (We exchanged waves with him the other day in the street but have not otherwise met him again.)

'Oh, nothing,' Mrs Spicer broke in. She sounded rather horrified at the question. 'He fell off a mountain in 1940. Hasn't been the same since.'

Somebody mentioned the name Brandon Brendon. It caused quite a stir. My ears pricked up. (He rang again this evening about bridge. Still couldn't understand a word he said.) Turns out he is headmaster of the American School here. All agreed it was 'a den of iniquity'. The pupils and staff spent their time lounging round smoking kif.

'If I had a son,' said Spicer, 'I'd even send him to the French School rather than that place!'

'He sets no example,' said Cassell, the vet. 'He's always drunk and smoking kif himself.'

'I used to be on the Parents' Association committee,' said the ex-nurse. 'But now he knows I'm against him, he won't allow me in the building.'

Someone else (not Mrs Spicer) said: 'It was all very idealistic in the beginning.'

'*It isn't any more!*' the rest chorused.

'But what can you do?' asked the vet hopelessly. 'The previous American Consul-General was as bad as Brendon and got withdrawn, and the new one is just under his thumb.'

Everyone concurred. Raymond, who had alone sat silent, now said in a low, confiding tone: 'You know Brendon goes on expensive tours of Africa with glossy brochures enticing the children of American diplomats from all over the Continent?' Raymond struck me as having the makings of a true biographer. He seemed to have the lowdown on everyone and everything in the Colony. He spoke little but always to great effect. He went on: 'After his tour, he goes back to Washington to raise funds. He spends about a day there, then has a month in Florida living it up on the money he's raised.'

'It's really iniquitous!' said the vet.

(Have sketched out five-day tour of Imperial Cities, leaving here Monday.)

17 January

Like yesterday: cold and cloudy. No commitments to the Colony (kind of rest day). Buried ourselves in the Claridge for lunch. French colonial décor: cane chairs, pink lamps on tables, silk canopy (*trompe l'œil*). Proved good food exists here. So it's curtains for the hotel restaurant.

Ate tonight at the Parade, which is old-style sleazy (Miss Stray put us onto it). Nice white building with pretty garden. You know at once the sort of place it is.

Inside: black-and-white tiles, arched alcoves, red plush. Pure pre-war Paris. At the bar: silk canopy (real); tarnished mirror behind, tarnished owner in front. Ex-bareback rider, nigh on ninety. Looks a year or two younger (and light years fiercer). Very raddled, very *Casablanca*. '*Marcel, fermez la porte!*' she rasps at the barman. He serves without speaking. Mostly without moving. As Miss Stray to the laugh like a drain, so Madame to the voice like gravel. (Tangier has taught me the truth of cliché.) When Madame speaks, you hear the crunch of hooves. Radio play policemen walking up drives.

We sit on high stools drinking dry martinis. Atmosphere of extreme tension. Madame nods to us (new customers, welcome). Dwarfish woman with huge nose serves Madame supper (old friend, loathed). Grand-scale resentment passes between them. Madame eats in silence. Sole sound yapping poodle beside her. She hands plate to it. Shoves her own at the barman.

Large American woman enters. Fur coat, bright red slacks. Lipstick to match. Orders vodka. Complains, 'Couldn't get a taxi.' Madame ignores her (old enemy, bored). Woman drinks vodka. Orders another. Grey, grizzled man enters. (Place is filling up.) *He* orders a vodka.

Besides us, one other diner. Elderly Englishman. Sits gloomily eating. Drinks a bottle with dinner, another with coffee. Speaks seldom, always in drunken slur. Clearly a regular.

It really is an enchanting place.

A state of siege today on the steps of the Tanja Flandria Hotel. Pests proffering all manner of junk at tourists trying to get out. The women fought furiously, the men hid behind, looking terrified. I thought I caught sight of the Pukka Quartet.

(Midnight.) It's turned out I did. But that, they've just told me, was the least of their troubles today. They were assaulted in the kasbah. Being pukka, they find it difficult to adopt a conciliatory tone with the Pests, who are therefore provoked. They found solace in the Claridge which I'd recommended to them. And tomorrow they go to Gib, which should be consoling.

It was. They came back glowing. Much taken by the 'little-bit-of-Britain-in-the-Med' aspects. Couldn't wait to sit down after dinner to watch Gib News on TV. This was especially incompetent tonight:

NEWSREADER: We will now see an interview with the new military commander.

(Pause. Nothing happens.)

NEWSREADER: I will move on to my next item... Today died at the age of 104 one of Gibraltar's leading artists.

(Picture of grizzled red-faced figure. It is the military commander.)

NEWSREADER: We apologise for the items not appearing in the right or—

(Voice of Newsreader cut off. Follows interview with deceased artist. He rants hysterically about Spanish realism. Intercut with barely visible stills of his paintings. Whenever these appear, his voice is superseded by another one which rants hysterically about naval defences. Finally both cut off and national anthem played to old print of Queen trooping colour.)

The Pukka Quartet are quite fun. They wear pin-stripe suits all day and dinner jackets in the evening. They go abroad together often, a kind of travelling British exhibition (Britain past, that is). They were in India last year where they said everyone was much more friendly and pro-British. Even in Moscow they were better treated than here. Their Russian guide asked if Britain had a health service. They said it did. But there was high unemployment in Britain, wasn't that true? They said it was. The guide said in Russia there was no unemployment: everyone was found a job. The Pukka Quartet said that in Britain, too, people could be *found* jobs. But they couldn't be made to *do* them. They could choose to remain unemployed. The guide said she believed them about the health service but not the rest. 'For, if you can be paid for not working, why should anyone work?'

The Pukka Quartet laughed heartily at this: if even communist Russians thought it absurd to pay people for not working, then why did the left-wingers at home call them 'fascist' for thinking the same?

I said compulsion was compulsion whatever name you gave it. It was better to pay a few people for not working than remedy a minor abuse at the cost of the general freedom.

They said: 'Yes, but we don't live in an ideal world...'

I said in an ideal world there would be no need of ideal solutions. It was only in this un-ideal one that they might serve a purpose.

They nodded but didn't seem persuaded.

(Have extended tour to eight days to include Marrakesh.)

19 January

Still unsettled.

We met Tommy Bidfine on the Boulevard, who said we must come and see him soon at Nettlewood. But hurried off without naming a date ('otherwise I'll catch my death!').

Have found a way of repelling the Pests (too late, alas, to benefit the Pukka Quartet, who went home today saying the threat of mugging at home would seem as nothing after this).

My remedy: you walk along prominently displaying a copy of *Matin du Sahara*. At once, the Pests give you a wide berth, sometimes even running away. There are two possible explanations for this. One is that they take you for a resident, long immune to their wiles. The other, more sinister, is that they see readers of the *Matin* as ardent *régimistes* likely to have them whipped off by the police (something all here are agreed is a fate worse than death).

This is not at all far-fetched. I got rid of one persistent Pest the other day just by rounding on him with the question, 'What do you think of the Sultan?' He was very frightened. Even talking to people generally here you find them extremely guarded on the subject of Hassan. The most you get is a cryptic 'Yes, people like the Sultan, but we think there will be a republic.' Apparently there are many groups plotting against him, especially among the young. (I would not like to be plotted against by these Pests.)

20 January

To Matins at St Andrew's. After heavy overnight rain, it was sunny as we strolled to the church which is just opposite the garden gates of the hotel. You step straight from the European atmosphere of sofas and armchairs into the bustling market and across Rue d'Angleterre stands the English Church: a subtle blend of English and Moroccan. In a hut at the entrance, a scribe writes letters and gives legal advice to anyone who pays. He arrives by taxi every morning.

We walked around the lush graveyard whose occupants testify to the benefits of this climate: three-digit ages frequent, few under ninety.

Inside the church, not much of a congregation, the weather perhaps keeping them away. The Waughs were there, and the Brigadier. No sign of the Spicers, or Miss Stray. The gas fire was pointed discreetly at the pew of the English Consul-General, even though he's away on leave. (As strangers we were greeted by the church warden, a woman called Miss Mare: tweed suit, brogues, brooch on lapel; what used to be termed a stickler.)

I'd forgotten how long the Anglican service is. I was soon nodding off. Kept awake by browsing the Book of Common Prayer about 'baptism of such as are of riper years' with 'parents or other discreet persons'. Also, 'visitation of the sick' ('the priest should encourage the sick to be liberal to the poor' – i.e. cough up in your will). And the list of forbidden couplings, a man with his 'father's father's wife', 'mother's father's wife', etc.

The vicar, Rev. Jones, looked washed-out. He has had twenty years in the Welsh valleys. The history of incumbents here is discouraging: one committed suicide, the last vanished in a typical boys scandal. Rev. Jones is filling in as locum. His sermon today was on Christian unity. (I heard Alec Waugh whisper, 'I'm not interested in all that. Why can't we leave the Papists to themselves? That's why we come here.') Rev. Jones was not very coherent. He tried to find links between Wales and Morocco. Described St David's in Pembrokeshire as 'a haven of peace' ('Certainly very dead,' someone observed on my right). He spoke of 'the seagulls, the seals, the Atlantic, the volcanic mountains, the seals, the...' I thought it would never end. Then, when it did, a small elderly American couple approached us in the aisle. I had heard them tell Rev. Jones they were 'passing through'. Now the woman went off while the husband – small, grey, squat, with spectacles tightly perched on his nose – gave me an evangelical harangue. There in the church and just after the service! What had I done to deserve this? 'Only the Lord can give salvation!' he raved. 'The sinner will be damned! It is clearly written in the Scriptures!' I brushed aside and with relief came out into the sunshine. He pursued, but I told him I was a Jehovah's Witness. He looked very shocked.

Rev. Jones, anxious to look after us, came up outside and told us the 'young people' meet at the Café de Paris every day at 11.30. This may have been a hint that we'd find none of them at church. 'Young' here is comparative. Someone at the Spicers referred to that Tommy Bidfine as a 'young blade'. He must be close to sixty.

'The Bishop told me you were coming,' Rev. Jones said, speaking in a slow Welsh lilt. 'I like him enormously. He seems to me a genuinely good man.' He spoke as though these had in his life been of rare occurrence. 'And he keeps up an enormous correspondence, despite the size of the diocese.' ('Diocese' is an understatement for the Bishop's preserve: an area encompassing the Roman Empire at its height.) Rev. Jones said that in all his years in Wales he'd never once had a letter from his Bishop. I suspect his soul-saving of others has been soul-destroying of himself. A kind man, I thought.

'You're writing then?' he suddenly asked me. 'Are you a journalist?'

'No. A writer.'

'Oh. A freelance, are you?'

'No. Just a writer.'

'Oh.' He looked dumbfounded. 'What's your theme?' he asked nervously.

The scene basked in British indomitability. Everyone looked

and behaved as if emerging from an English country church on a bright morning of mid-summer. It may be that all national arrogance has the capacity on occasion to rise above the fatuities of chauvinism, but standing in that churchyard looking around, I asked myself why the British kind seemed so particularly disarming, why these people even now, though a minority of a minority, could get away with acting as if they were in total possession of the place. The reason is exactly what ought to rouse most hostility: because what allows the British kind of arrogance to acquit itself like this is its sense of its own absurdity, its self-mockery, its cynical ability to let others take seriously just those things it finds funny about itself. And the more adverse the circumstances in which this arrogance is asserted, the more sublime its self-conscious absurdity. It was at its best in 1940; is at its worst in the endless nostalgia for 1940, which by protesting too much casts doubt on the original heroism.

As I ruminated along these lines, a French woman called Nina came up to us and said: 'This afternoon I will take you to see Phoenician tombs and give you tea on the Mountain.' (Perhaps there is something in Spicer's Francophobia.)

After church, we set off with the Waughs as we'd arranged. Alec wore a fur hat and a black overcoat with an astrakhan collar taken from an old coat given him by Michael Arlen. I told him the fur hat was more Moscow than Tangier. 'Yes,' he agreed, 'but I'm wearing an MCC tie to redress the balance.' En route I bought my *Matin du Sahara* as usual. Waugh also bought a copy: 'I follow the cartoon serial.' I said I followed the S.M. serial.

We walked to Madame Porte's Salon de Thé off the Boulevard, one of the three places – the Claridge and the Parade Bar the other two – on which we've rung the changes. Drinks at Porte's, dinner at the Claridge, coffee at the Parade; drinks at Porte's, dinner at the Parade, coffee at the Claridge; drinks at Porte's, dinner *and* coffee at the Parade/Claridge. Porte's shuts at eight so no dinner or coffee is possible there. Far cry from the days when Tangier boasted dining out that put cities in Europe to shame.

Madame Porte herself – a notorious Vichyiste – is no more, but the place retains all the character she imposed on it: straight out of *Casablanca*, cross between old-style English department store and Parisian night-club of the Twenties. It's become a haunt of the Spanish colony: men in black, women in furs and pearls, hair long, and Goya faces. Also Moroccan businessmen in conference, keeping their voices low, and Moroccan gays keeping theirs high. A mixture of the elegant and the bohemian such as has all but disappeared from Europe – certainly north of the Alps, where the choice now is between the flashy and the proletarian.

We sit over the famous – and deadly – martinis served in tall hock glasses with little cheese biscuits (very good). Alec Waugh gets neat square ham sandwiches: he's publicised the place in his books. As we drink, he points out a dagoish figure with a large bright moustache across the way. 'That's the grandson of Rassaouli,' he says. 'You know – who kidnapped *The Times* correspondent, W B Harris.' 'I sold him my car,' says Virginia. 'The grandson, I mean.' Virginia is much lighter today, less defensive, more forthcoming. She is not well, suffering from the effects of an aneurysm: her mood of the other night probably accountable to that. In her bucket hat she still suggests the American Women's Institute or Literary Guild or something: a matron from the Mid-West. But she was lively and much happier to let the talk wander, perhaps having decided we were 'all right' for Alec: something I'm afraid neither of us had ever doubted.

He was very entertaining. Everything he says is delivered easily, the flowing geniality punctuated only by a wry smile at the end – e.g. '…a Yorkshireman and didn't play cricket. Didn't take to him.' (Wry smile.)

In the last year or so, I've met four elderly writers, all well known; two eminent. Of them Alec Waugh is the most amiable, the least intellectual, by far the most serene.

We went by taxi to Guitta's, a restaurant near the Place Kowait (by day bland and dusty, with none of the nightmarish quality it had for us when we were stumbling bemusedly round it looking for the Waughs' apartment). The restaurant served an 'English-style' Sunday lunch: bœuf bourgignon followed by zabaglione. The Waughs didn't think this very English. But they don't come to England now.

Alec spoke amusingly about his contemporaries (including Evelyn) but I felt G knew more about them than he did. G's knowledge of inter-war literary life never ceases to astound me. At one point, Waugh himself said: 'Virginia, this young man knows more about me than you do!' I don't imagine there can be many 25-year-olds who are able to talk fluently about the likes of Hugh Kingsmill and Brian Lunn.

During this, Waugh made an attempt to explain why he came to live abroad after the war. Partly it was the austerity of England at the time. ('You couldn't get anything – not even a suit.') Partly he felt a slight coolness towards him on account of his success in America. (That period was also, of course, a high point of his brother's reputation.)

Finally saw Brandon Brendon (Brendon Brandon? – still not sure), headmaster of the American School and our persistent bridge-playing caller. He was giving lunch to a wizened elderly man called the Honourable Someone or other, relative of a marquess or duke of somewhere (Hereford? Or am I thinking of Spicer's origins? Can never recall titles).

Brendon is a bloated, dishevelled, altogether clapped-out looking man of, oh, at least thirty-two, I should say. His face (unique in my experience) quite *serrated*, but happily hidden by a mass of black hair that falls chaotically over it. He spoke in a loud semi-coherent voice (in contrast to his guest, who said little throughout their meal apart from an occasional 'Hello, darling' to someone passing the table). By the end of it, Brendon was hopelessly drunk and addressing the entire restaurant about some music festival he was running in spring. A terrible sight.

As we left, Alec Waugh did a little dance along the pavement. He said we must meet again soon.

Back at the hotel, the Frenchwoman Nina was waiting for us ('*quarter* to three'). Like everyone here, excessively punctual. We set off at once for the Phoenician tombs. The weather had turned cloudy again with a distinct hint of rain, and away from the shelter of Tangier it was very windy. But from Nina's determined, organised manner, you got the impression that a full-scale hurricane would not prevent us.

In the front passenger seat of the car sat an old man with a stick, a jittery eighty-year-old (his frailty all the more noticeable to us having just come from the sprightly octogenarian Waugh).

This was Esmé St Clair – he of whom the rubber sculpture was made in which Bidfine and Raymond smuggle in whiskey from Ceuta. (Also I recalled Miss Stray mentioning someone she refers to as 'Chase Me Esmee'. Presumably the same person. She had once shared a flat with him. They have not been seen since at the same functions.)

Nina is companion to the 95-year-old mentioned at the Spicers' – who had travelled to London and back on a bus: Mrs Févier. Her dog Lusty (whose 'walk' this trip was to be) was in the back of the car between G and me and frisked about, discarding hairs all over us. 'It's a very *in*telligent dog,' Nina observed, throwing us a protective cloth as we drove out west of Tangier into the rolling hills. 'It *can* fetch any species *of* flower from the garden complete with name *tag*.' Nina's English is fluent but spoken with a heavy French accent and a curiously syncopated stress. We tried not to draw her attention too much as she has the habit when driving of turning to speak rather than addressing you through the mirror. In any case, we were too busy fending off Lusty, which was vigorously living up to its name.

'It's a very racist dog,' Esmé explained. 'It's only friendly to Europeans. In the street it chases Moroccans. Even from the car it growls at them. Your sun-tans are confusing it.'

Luckily it was only a fifteen-minute drive. We got out at a beach beside the remains of the Phoenician settlement. The Atlantic was quite rough and with the strong wind and flickering sunlight through scudding clouds the atmosphere suggested a fine summer day in Cornwall.

Nina and I set off in front, G following with Esmé. In view of the latter's condition, I had not mentioned the state of my own foot, which was still hurting a little. But Nina, making no allowance at all for Esmé's necessarily slow rate of progress, strode off at the furious pace Lusty was setting at the end of the lead. I could see the dog's walk getting out of hand, so suggested we slow down a bit for Esmé, casually adding that I had a bit of a gammy foot myself.

'Oh? How *did* you do it?' Nina asked. 'Were you drunk? But I hope you won't use it as an *ex*cuse to do no*thing*,' she went on, without adjusting her speed in the slightest.

We scrambled over rubble, accompanied now by a monk-like

Moroccan who hung about the place in hope of a few dirhams from anyone mad enough to come there on a day like this. Muffled up in his djellaba and hood he was barely audible as in rather basic Spanish he made a few self-evident remarks about the bits and pieces we were so swiftly passing. 'Really? *How* interesting,' Nina would remark, turning to add to me: 'I don't know what *on* earth he has said, do you, Gregory?' She seemed quite unable to distinguish between the two of us, switching our names with a timing which could not be perfected even in the artifice of fiction. 'I am *a*fraid John will be tied to Esmé,' she said to me now. 'Still, we cannot wait *for* them.'

Looking back, I could see that Esmé had actually given up after only a few steps. G had caught us up.

'Ah, look, Gregory, here is John coming now.'

For an hour or so we rummaged among the Phoenician ruins. It seemed an odd thing to be doing on a Sunday afternoon of mid-winter a thousand miles from home. The wild invigorating beauty of the scene contrasted with the melancholy, derelict air of the rain-filled tombs. I was beginning to think the derelict Tangier's speciality. More than anything, its latterday character is set by crumbling people and places. Curiously, I am finding a kind of exhilaration in that: because, in spite of it, enormous vitality survives here. Most of the contemporary world is derelict in one way or another. It's easy to be deluded by a high standard of living into thinking otherwise about your own corner of it, for all the surrounding evidence of decay. Observing the low standard of living in a poor country only confirms that view, whereas the dereliction is more widespread than we are led to believe. To be stumbling around on a gusty afternoon among the ruins of one civilisation puts into perspective the tawdry nature of our own.

We drove on towards Cap Spartel in the glowing late sunshine, the hills very green despite the drought which has ended only these last few days. At one point the Atlantic and Mediterranean were visible together. But just as the drive was becoming interesting, Nina remembered a phone call from Paris she was expecting at five. It was now a quarter to. 'Would you turn the car round for me, John?' she asked Greg. 'My left arm *is* weak and I have *only* one good eye.' These revelations came at a bad moment, since Nina now drove at breakneck speed back to the Février house on the Mountain. (This is of course just a wide-ranging hill, the 'Old' side looking seawards, the 'New' facing Tangier.)

The Février Villa is grand in the between-the-wars Riviera style. It was built (like the one next door – now inhabited by the Governor of Tangier) by the (French) father-in-law of the 95-year-old Edie Février, with whom Nina has been now for almost ten years. Esmé's position in the household is less clear. He came there after the unsuccessful experiment with Miss Stray ('Couldn't get on,' he explained shortly).

As at the Spicers' (only plusher) everything in the house suggested the Home Counties – even a log fire. The sub-tropical garden and the view of Tangier from the terrace alone destroyed the illusion of being somewhere in Sussex which we felt as we sat in the expansive drawing-room on chintz-covered sofas sipping Lipton's tea and nibbling sponge-cake. But for all its spaciousness and airiness, the place had an oppressive feel. A dominating presence hung over it, constraining conversation. Nina – perhaps being used to it – chattered about the house and Mrs Février. (Her call had not materialised though we were back there by five.) Esmé said little. He looked depressed and certainly his physical condition gives him cause enough. He is very frail and shaky. 'I have a problem of balance,' he explained in a voice reminiscent of John Gielgud's. He speaks in a rather over-enunciated way and his tongue lingers between his lips as he hesitates over words. He is quite tall and slim, probably dashing and handsome in youth. But now only the watery pale-blue eyes and occasional broad smile (that lightens an otherwise much-fallen face) suggest any former distinction.

Now and then, a voice off could be heard but neither Nina nor Esmé paid it any attention. Sometimes it rose to a shrill imperative and a word or two of English – 'at once!' or 'shut up!' – could just be made out. More often the sounds were mere squawks of exasperation. I guessed from Nina's description that Mrs Février must be the source of these cries. At length the door opened and a servant entered pushing her before him in her wheelchair. She sat for a moment, like a child seeing new faces, contemplating the scene; then said:

'Why wasn't I informed we have guests?'

'I *imagined* you were still having *your* siesta,' Nina replied, completing unhurriedly the refilling of our tea-cups on which she was engaged. She then paused to introduce us.

'Delighted to meet you,' Mrs Févier said in a tone so much friendlier than the one she had used on Nina that it sounded altogether like a different person. Mrs Févier's voice was still resonant and she looked considerably younger than Esmé (who it turns out is not seventy, even). All this was deceptive though of her real condition, which soon became clear.

'Why aren't you having tea on the terrace?' she asked Nina, reverting to the severe manner.

'It's *too* cold.'

'Not for them it won't be. They're young,' said Mrs Févier, nodding at us.

'For Esmé and me then it is *too* cold.'

'You mustn't think only of yourselves,' Mrs Févier observed. Nina, who had told us Mrs Févier did nothing but that, remained silent. To me, Mrs Févier said sweetly: 'From the terrace there is a beautiful view of the Malvern Hills.'

'Really?' I said. 'I thought it was the Sierra Nevada…'

Mrs Févier laughed: 'Did you hear that? This young man thinks you can see the mountains of Spain from here! He must be mad—'

Beside me Esmé tottered proffering the sponge-cake. 'No idea where she is or anything,' he muttered.

'We had Sir Charles Grandison and Miss Herbert Byron to lunch,' Mrs Févier went on.

'Oh, don't be so *ridiculous*!' Nina said forcefully. 'Those are chara*cters* in the nov*el* I was reading you yest*er*day.' In this mood Nina's intonation went completely to pieces, her stresses all over the place.

Mrs Févier ignored the interruption. 'A charming man, Sir Charles,' she continued. 'And he and Miss Byron are clearly very much in love. But Sir Charles is pledged to a noble Italian lady, their difference of religion alone preventing a union. The lady is distracted with unhappiness, to such an extent that her parents are prepared to give way over the religious question. But should they do so, and the wedding take place, Miss Byron will be mortified.'

'I expect it'll all turn out well in the end,' said Esmé; adding to me: 'It usually does in Richardson.' He gave his broad smile and his tongue hovered between his lips. Seeing Mrs Févier seemed to have cheered him up, perhaps by reminding him that, for all the wreckage of his face and body, he was still compos mentis. ('Just,' he told me later.)

'Take *no* notice of her,' said Nina. 'She refers all *the* time to characters from the books *I* read her and talks about scenes *in* them as if they were events in *her* life. It is very try*ing*. Would you like some tea, Edie, or *have* you had some?' she asked her charge.

'I had tea the other day,' said Mrs Févier slowly, 'in a country house with a Miss Gwendoline Fairfax. I found her a most rude and disagreeable person.'

'It's *quite* hopeless to entertain here,' said Nina. 'Where is that phone call *of* mine?'

I was struck by the irony of fate that had brought together these two formidable women, about whom there was more symmetry than sympathy. The French Nina had married an English husband, the English Edie a French one. But Nina had a French name (Dupresne) and Edie an English one: the former's husband coming from a Dorset family with old French connections, the latter's from a Normandy line with old English ones. The two widows, who in age were more than thirty years apart, were in background alike: daughters of colonial parents – Edie's in India, Nina's in North Africa. When Morocco became independent, Nina returned with her parents to France but found it intolerable and after the death of her husband and an experiment with England, accepted the post with Mrs Févier in Tangier. Edie has been in Tangier since 1905 when her parents stopped here on the way back from India and, finding even this climate cool, decided to go no further. (Raymond, the biographer of Harris, told us he came upon a newspaper of that year announcing 'the arrival from Gibraltar of Mr and Mrs Gardener and their daughter Edith'.)

With a natural endowment of one set of national traits, each woman appears to have picked up by marriage the other's. The result is a devastating ability to ignore all distractions and setbacks and plough on remorselessly with a single-minded purpose. So

Nina could analyse aloud all the reasons why her phone call from Paris had not materialised at the same time as Mrs Févier outlined famous scenes from fiction as the chronicle of her recent life.

'...and that I *know* is true,' she was saying about a wedding she had attended which, though I'd not read it for some years, I had an idea was from *Jane Eyre*.

'*Of* course it is not true!' Nina put in, momentarily pausing to administer this rebuke but instantly returning to her own obsessive topic: '*To* think that my son has *par*ticularly said he would ring me at five o'clock today *from* Paris and here is more than half past five and still *no* call!'

'You have to remember the time difference,' Esmé observed. He looked very worn out by all this.

'But Paris is one hour *a*head!' Nina protested. 'There it is now *half* past six!'

'It *is* true,' Mrs Févier continued, addressing G and myself, 'because I saw it on the social page of *The Times!*' She laughed quietly in triumph over this, then turning to Nina said in a languid, desultory tone, as though referring to a matter of no great consequence: 'The phone rang at four o'clock. Nobody answered it.'

Nina drove us half-way back to Miss Stray's where we were due (*quarter* to seven) for what she calls 'pre-drinks drinks'. Nina was invited but pleaded a headache (i.e. Mrs Févier); Esmé of course wasn't. So there were just ourselves and Brigadier Hasta.

Miss Stray's flat – on the airy, elegant Marshan: the Hampstead of Tangier – is the ground floor of a house in a pretty little 19th-century terrace (straight out of Kensington). It looks across a broad street to a small park beyond which stands the football stadium (not at all an undistinguished building, with a nice Moorish entrance). The flat is run-down in an old colonial way: grubby white walls, shabby curtains, a few sticks of crumbling furniture; mementoes and photographs strewn around, scarves and turbans hanging on hooks. Couldn't have been more different from the Févier villa. It had genuine style.

Miss Stray had donned a few beads for the occasion. Sported a cigarette holder and wore what looked like an old-fashioned tea-gown but might have been a cut-down djellaba. She gave us beers 'to start', then tottered back and forth to the kitchen organising kir with wine and a dish or two of peanuts. ('No Porte's biscuits; cheque's late this month.')

She apologised for the lack of gin.

'Best bet's the boat to Gib,' the Brigadier suggested on the subject of price.

'Yes, but you've got to pay still to get on it,' Miss Stray objected.

'There's a half-price return on a Friday.'

'Still too much for this gal.'

The Brigadier said the alcohol question would be the one thing to make him consider moving. 'But then where would one go? I'd like to live in Italy – but it's impossible now. Oh, not because of the chaos and whatever. There's chaos everywhere these days. But you have to pay the earth for some little hut or whatever and they expect you to do it up and turn it into a palace and probably let people walk around it umpteen times a year. And besides, you can't get servants – not good ones anyway. No, Italy's a place to visit. And I love visiting it.'

He said he stayed often on lake Orta with a former Dutch ambassadress to Belgium. 'I was military-attaché in Brussels when I met her. She has a house on that lovely island in the lake. Her husband was the acme of diplomatic protocol. Every knife in its place at dinner and so forth. She's quite the opposite – complete bohemian. Had to split up. Anyhow – one evening – four of us to dinner – all sitting on the terrace – Madame spies a bird below in the water struggling for its life. "Oh, Giovanni! Do something!" she cries—' (the Brigadier gestured dramatically with his glass; I shifted slightly; have only one spare pair of trousers) '—Giovanni's the butler – young, good-looking chap,' he added reminiscently. 'So – few minutes pass, then Giovanni appears stripped down to swimming trunks. Dives into water, retrieves bird. Short interval. Reappears. Immaculately dressed again. Goes on serving dinner. *That's* the kind of servant one wants,' he concluded wistfully; he fixed his eyes on his drink, the good one reflecting its sparkle, the pink one its colour.

Miss Stray asked how we liked the hotel. 'The Bish always stays there when he comes. I'm the Bish's best friend in Tangier. He's a lovely man. I adore him. He confirmed me. It was just after he was made Bish. I was nervous and he said, "Don't worry, I'm a new girl myself".' She took a gulp of her drink which, as the cistern flushed simultaneously, provoked a literal overflow. Stemming the tide, she went on: "Course, Miss Mare is the Bish's great enemy. Have you met Miss Mare? Known to her friends as the Nag.'

'And to her enemies as the Steam Roller,' the Brigadier put in.

I said we'd been welcomed by her this morning at church.

'Yes, that's her usual hangout,' Miss Stray drawled, surprisingly drily.

I asked why Miss Mare didn't get on with the Bishop.

'Oh, she's against anyone who's against ordination of women. Which really means ordination of *her*. Got a great ambition to be a preacher.'

'I should think her best bet's marrying the vicar,' said Brigadier Hasta.

'She's working on it,' Miss Stray said. 'She's desperate to get men up to that mansion of hers. Night*mare* Abbey I call it. Tell all m' men friends to keep clear. Like entering the terminal ward. Never come out alive.'

'But d'you think Rev. Jones would be interested?' the Brigadier asked before Miss Stray's cistern had a chance to refill. 'He seems a very quiet, well-mannered kind of man.'

'Yes, he *is* unusual,' said Miss Stray. 'Normally vicars here have a specialist interest: poor boys or rich gals.'

'We find they alternate,' the Brigadier explained. 'You never get two of the same kind on the trot.'

'Yes. They either commit suicide or marry a fortune.'

'There was quite a scandal with the last one.'

'And an even bigger one with the one before last!'

'Oh dear, *yes*. The unfortunate Reverend Shiftey.'

'Certainly lived up to his name,' said Miss Stray, adding, 'Shifted pretty quick when the police arrived too.' She lifted her drink but the glass was empty so the drain soon dried up.

'He did say some foolish things,' the Brigadier conceded. 'And people *listen* to a vicar.'

'First I've heard of it,' Miss Stray said, replenishing glasses all round. 'It was all Sleeping Beauties last Sunday.'

'Even so, I've a feeling Rev. Jones is too good for this world,' the Brigadier reflected.

'He's more than that: he's too good for Tangier,' Miss Stray observed.

'Well, at least he's only here as a locum.'

'The Nag moves quicker than her name implies.' (Full flush of the cistern.)

'So you're going away, are you?' asked the Brigadier (when the noise had died down). 'Driven you mad, have we? We usually do.'

I said we'd be back in a week or two.

'Are you going to Fez?' Miss Stray asked. 'It's a lovely place. I went there once,' she immediately added.

'You should see Harvey Lambert in Fez,' said the Brigadier.

'Yes, you should,' said Miss Stray. 'He's a lamb. Only got one eye.'

The Brigadier said he hoped we'd get to Marrakesh. I said we were starting there.

'I've had good times in Marrakesh,' Miss Stray said in a nostalgic tone of voice. 'Used to get driven down there in an open-topped Rolls. Champagne picnics. All that.' She sat for a moment staring into her glass, as if it were a crystal ball of the past rather than the future.

G asked her to recommend a hotel.

'Oh, don't ask *me*!' she said, spluttering her drink in indignation. 'I haven't been there for twenty years!'

'They've all gone off,' said the Brigadier sadly.

Suddenly Miss Stray cheered up again. We had another round of drinks. 'Give my love to the Auck,' she said. 'If he's still alive and not as gaga as they say.'

The Brigadier said he thought General Auckinleck might be showing his ninety-odd years. 'He was a marvellous commander. Montgomery got all the credit but he did all the work. Always had an eye for a sortie.'

'*And* for a soldier!' Miss Stray added. 'They say his villa is like Buckingham Palace: they're always changing the guard!'

('It's a great pity,' said the Brigadier as he drove us back, 'there just aren't the amusing people there once were in Tangier.')

We fly to Marrakesh tomorrow.

Part Two

Tangier

5 February

(Midnight.)
Arrived back an hour ago. On the 'rapide' from Fez (hundred and fifty miles in five hours).

Like coming home. Room aired, windows open to soft night air (spring has come in our absence); chicken and white wine supper on the table – best meal we've had here; the Beethoven sonatas playing.

Letter waiting from Nina. Says much has happened while we've been away...
  ?

6 February

(Dawn.)
Two weeks of impressions to get down – before it all gets going again...

Have had little time to write during the tour. What I did scribble down – on trains, in cafés – have mostly torn up: scrappy and incoherent. As usual, the crucial things stand out in retrospect.

General impressions: mainly of meals and medinas. Seemed always to be having one or doing the other. Of the meals I recall delicious brochettes with gris de Boulamane on a nondescript boulevard in Meknès; terrible alcohol-less cous-cous beneath banana trees in Fez; and an idyllic lunch-by-the-pool spent fighting off wasps in Marrakesh. These the highlights of the trip just because of their mixed blessings. Like wrong-note harmonies and resorts out of season, they had the off-key quality that leaves a stronger impression than perfection.

There *were* perfect meals in perfect settings, but as so often they exist in a glow – like conventional images of heaven, too vague and amorphous to have much sense of reality, losing with time even their ability to convince you they happened.

As for imperfect meals in imperfect settings (of which there were plenty) their mediocrity makes them unmemorable. Only the full-scale disaster has anything to recommend it. And of these we had – alas – but one.

It took place at a restaurant in Marrakesh called *Chez Jack' Line* (sic).

We were drawn in from a chilly evening by the sight of candles on the table and sole meunière on the menu ('menu' in the French sense: our table d'hôte). A fat, unintelligible waiter urged us to have the plat du jour. Could not make out from his mutterings what this was. Went ahead with the menu.

To start, we were brought a tomato with a knob of something on top. I glanced at the list: 'salmon salad'. Apprehensive, we continued. Next came a minute portion, which at first I thought was the butter we had asked for. Turned out to be 'cheese omelette'. We mentioned the sole meunière. The waiter waved his arms and, resetting our dirty cutlery for the second time, went into that hotch-potch of sounds which some waiters, seeing you are foreign, resort to in the hope that a few of them may correspond to your native tongue. Of course, exactly the reverse is the case: you can't make out a thing they are saying. Whereas if they stuck to their own language, you would – however ignorant of it you were – probably get the gist of their meaning.

Some noisy music began at this moment so it was impossible to hear anyway. The waiter took out a stump of pencil and put a line through everything on the menu. Was nothing then available, I asked in French. He replied by performing a series of mimes designed to suggest some animal that was. In the style of which he then – before I could demand fresh cutlery – ran off; returning some time later with two plates of bones in a pool of grease, 'garni' (sic the menu) with an upturned cup of rice.

I called the manager. A figure of uncertain sex appeared. Carrot-coloured hair, stage make-up, pink high-heeled shoes: a cross between a man in drag and the keeper of a Belle Epoque brothel. Told her (approximate pronoun) to take away the disgusting rabbit (which she insisted it was), bring us the *à la carte* and we should start again. She said it was never advisable to have the tourist menu. I said in that case perhaps she could advise her customers by not placing it prominently in the window. She would then anticipate the withdrawal of the corresponding tax benefits and rate reductions which would follow my registering a complaint with the tourist authority. (Of course, nothing of the kind will occur: the relevant bribe had either been paid or was about to be. But you have to go through the motions.)

Those meals – good or ill – in the worldly modern quarters always came as a reward for the medinas. As did the gardens in Marrakesh: a true Arab paradise after the purgatory of the medina (no, the *hell of life on earth* of the medina). In their tranquillity you could enjoy the *recollection* of the medina – much as people hope to relive in heaven those celebrated moments of intensity too transient to appreciate at the time.

But *in* the medina I felt like the Henry James characters who complain of the weary hours and days they spend 'in the cars'. I see them now, those medinas, as a kind of endurance test, a version of running the gauntlet.

First the sights. Traipsing round mosque and medersa I thought again of those Jamesian tourists with their Baedeckers. It was not exactly the 'seen one, seen them all' school of thought (someone's judgment here – the Brigadier's? I forget); just the mesmerising effect of repetition.

Then the Pests of course. You get rid of them by hiring a Guide. Which is where your problems begin.

However good and well-intentioned the Guide, and however much (and often) you remonstrate, you know your path will inevitably lead to a shop; and probably to more than one.

In Marrakesh, for all our protestations and assurances that we would not buy, we were taken to see 'an artist' who made 'pieces of art' in his 'spare time', after he had completed his latest 'commission' (many certificates, many pictures with notable customers, many expressions of unparalleled excellence). 'Nothing for sale; all for himself. Come not to buy. Only for watch and admire.' We watch and admire. Artist sits crouched over Koran copying out decorative motifs onto tray. Artist smiles at us. We smile back, murmur more praises. Artist mumbles friendly words to Guide with nod towards us. 'He says he likes you. Allah loves you.' We are appreciative. We bestow thanks. 'He says for you he wishes something special.' We are overwhelmed. 'He says for you he will *sell* pieces of his art. Normally, no. But for you, yes.' We express our amazement, are sad that we cannot afford so great an honour. 'He says for you he makes *special price*. You are first of day over threshold. Also is low season.'

In Fez, the Guide, in response to our pleas, said 'No shops'. Instead, at the end of our very thorough tour, we will visit beautiful 'grand house of medina converted to new use'. By an extraordinary coincidence beautiful grand house of medina has been converted into carpet shop.

We are welcomed by the dagoish kind of Moroccan you see in the most expensive London nightclubs. White leather jacket, tailored denim jeans, silk shirt, pointed patent leather shoes. Well-heeled in every sense. He seats us, gives us mint tea ('not for business, you understand'). Claps hands. Minions roll out carpets. Berber carpets ('plain, not expensive'). Arab carpets ('Fine. Not *very* expensive'). Vintage carpets ('Not for purchase. Piece of art').

However, for us...

First over threshold? I enquire.

Yes, today we are first over—

Low season?

Yes... very low season... 'But in high season has come Henry Kissinger with entire entourage, spend ten thousand dirhams, say of all Arab cities Fez only has heart.' (I hear the voice of an aide: You're in *Fez* today, Henry.)

Seeing we know the score, proprietor drops strident salesman line, lapses into idiomatic English. 'I been to England, I seen the prices – in South Kensington, in Harrod's.' Yes, we can't afford those either. Anyway we live in Walworth. ('Is that near South Kensington?')

G goes into some detail about our finances. Very embarrassing. Only here thanks to bank manager's kindness and so on. Proprietor most sympathetic. (Guide forlorn: how did he end up with this pair of duds?) Proprietor amazed that after years of study and practice English doctor can't afford Moroccan carpet. (Quite shocked myself to hear the full horror of it.) If the tourists are broke, what hope for Moroccans?

All sit sipping mint tea, staring at rolled out carpets. Proprietor offers cigarettes. (Guide beginning to look worried about fee.) Shake hands, embrace, touching farewells. Proprietor says always happy to see us in Morocco. We say he is welcome in Walworth. 'Inch' Allah,' he says sadly. 'Inch' Allah,' we repeat. ('Inch' Bank Manager,' we add to ourselves.)

Much more to report but St Andrew's bell is tolling. For whom doth it toll?

(Noon.)
For Mrs Févier. A memorial service. Her death has been the main event in our absence.

I couldn't make out Rev. Jones' prayer for her. Something about a sacrifice rather than a loss. (The old man next to me heard 'cross': 'What's he mean? She was like the Saviour or a terrible burden?')

Everyone was at the memorial service. (She was a great bastion of the church. Gave generously. Has presumably done so in her will.) But the event seemed less a mark of her passing than a celebration of the other big news: Rev. Jones and Miss Mare have announced their engagement!

According to Esmé St Clair (who invited us to lunch at the Févier villa, saying it would be 'easier' now) they went off on an eight-day tour and 'found one another' ('They can't have been looking very hard'). They also found a Roman coin ('It was numismatology at first sight'). I talked about it with Rev. Jones after the service (Miss Mare hovered in the background). 'It happened at Volubilis,' he began, and for a second I thought he was describing the romance. But then he mentioned a Cleopatra head and I knew it wasn't Miss Mare we were speaking of. 'Cleopatra married the first King of Morocco,' he explained. 'By rights of course the coin should go to the Government...' He seemed embarrassed, said: 'Would you like to come to Asilah with us tomorrow – for the Festival of the Mouled? Miss Mare says they put on quite a show there...'

(I enquired of people about the Hubert-Smythes today – those 'eccentric' politics of theirs have nagged my curiosity these past weeks. But unfortunately they've gone to Paris and may not be back before we leave… Meanwhile, that Brandon Brendon – or vice versa – rang up again about bridge. As usual, incoherent. Did I play Blockwood?)

7 *February*

Our trip to Asilah – a little fishing village about thirty miles south – with Rev. Jones and Miss Mare.

We didn't recognise him at first ('Why? Was he in drag?' asked Miss Stray when I told her this evening. Prolonged drainage). The reason was that, despite the warmth of the day, he wore a raincoat, thick black trousers and sweater and, with woollen hat and dark glasses, looked the model of a cat burglar. Seeing our looks of surprise he pointed to the woollen hat, as if that alone needed explaining, and said: 'I've little hair, you see. Useful for the evening chill.' He is turning out an interesting character. (A thing you find a lot with people here.)

Miss Mare must be in her late fifties; very forthright and no-nonsense but smiles and has an almost literally agreeable manner, nodding all the time you speak and throwing in an 'Oh yes!' or 'Definitely!' Even so, you feel disagreement with her might be a problem.

On the road she drove very fast and, considering that like all roads here it was deserted, with amazing disregard for the few drivers we met. 'Get out of the way, can't you? Why are you going so *slowly*?' All the time keeping up a running commentary on the scenery (almond blossom; gently rolling, almost English hills; occasional herd of camels). She has lived all her life in Morocco. This has not though stopped her being hyper-British; has if anything encouraged it, as so often with Britons left to long maturation in the sun. While the home product adapts to the changing climate, the foreign-based variety just goes on ripening.

Miss Mare's account of what we were going to see was very much 'heathens at play': 'Celebration of Prophet's birth – get themselves all worked up – dance all day – finally go into trance – probably all on hashish—'

Asilah we'd already visited on our own: pretty little place with new quarter built by the Spanish. Portuguese kasbah; ramparts with good view of the Atlantic; *sight* – Rassaouni's Palace (closed).

When we asked Alec Waugh what to see he looked puzzled. Said: 'You go there for lunch.' He was right. We had a very good lunch, under the walls of the kasbah by the sea in bright warm sunshine. Freshly caught sole brought to the table; golden white wine.

Then it couldn't have been sleepier. Today it was bustling with life. Although we'd seen what there was to see, we concurred politely when Miss Mare offered to show us round before the festivities got going in earnest. She made straight for the medina and hailed a 'guide' ('Keeps the boys at bay').

The 'guide' – a middle-aged man – wore a three-piece pinstripe suit and polo-neck sweater under his djellaba. He spoke English like Warren Beatty. He was very obviously otherwise engaged but naturally not going to turn up a chance like this. His remarks, like most guides', were few and fatuous. 'This is very old... this place sells jewellery – jewellers work here.' I asked to see Rassaouni's Palace. 'Is clozèd.' He said this with satisfaction; as usual his aim was to get us to a shop for commission.

In this he was assisted when Miss Mare broke the heel of her shoe. ('I always break shoes. I break them wherever I go. I once broke a shoe in Brazil.') The guide was all courtesy – 'No problem' – and quickly steered us to a shop. This was called the Arts and Crafts School, which I knew from Fez meant carpets. I disappeared to the lavatory while Miss Mare had her shoe seen to. Was horrified to come back and find everyone seated and a man diligently rolling out carpets. It was Fez all over again. I asked the others if they wanted this. They shook their heads. Miss Mare returned to her shoe. I explained to the owner that we were on a guided tour. We wouldn't be buying. 'But no need to buy!' came the typical reply. 'We explain *for* guided tour kind of Moroccan carpet. For interest in country.' This was a new one but I was up to it. 'We've had the lecture,' I said, 'in Fez – Meknès – Rabat – Marrakesh – we've seen thousands of carpets!'

'Oh – you have been in many places,' he said warily, making a sign behind his back. No joy here, he was thinking, and swiftly the staff, responding to the signal, were swinging down leather bags instead. These they deposited on the Rev. Jones who made the kind of ritually encouraging sounds he had probably used throughout life at parish jumble sales.

Meanwhile the younger members of staff took Greg and me aside and talked about football. They examined each other's thighs. One, missing both front teeth (dentistry doesn't seem too hot here), felt my right thigh. 'This not for football,' he said. 'This for sleeping with.' At his invitation I felt his.

'Very good for football,' I said.

'Also for sleeping,' he replied silkily. (Through the corner of my eye I could see Miss Mare showing interest in something. 'They're very good value,' she was saying.)

The gap-toothed boy asked if I would like to sleep with him. Not wanting to hurt his feelings I said yes, but some other time. Another boy took me into a cubicle and showed me pouffes. I expressed huge indifference to them. He shook his head. 'Not for buy – for make more comfortable,' he said, with a glance at my trousers. (Through the bead curtains of the cubicle I caught a glimpse of a third boy in the one next door measuring G's inside leg. Or that's what it looked like.)

My boy started taking his clothes off. Outside Miss Mare was haggling over prices. I was sure this would be an issue on our side as well. The shopkeeper, seeing all his customers happy, brought us mint tea. I said I thought this was going to cost money. He said no, mint tea was on the house. I said I wasn't referring to the tea. The gap-toothed boy (who had entered) said: 'Only a leetle!' I made ritual remarks about in England sex being free. 'Also in Morocco!' said the now near-nude boy. ('I hope we're not keeping you!' Rev. Jones called.) 'For Moroccans,' I said to the boy, 'not for foreigners.'

'Ah, but foreign peoples bring diseases,' said the gap-toothed boy sadly. 'We have to pay for treatment. So must insure ourselves.'

This seemed so eminently sensible (a kind of self-service BUPA) I was almost persuaded. But just then a cry of triumph rang out from Miss Mare. 'He came right down from ninety to thirty!' I heard her tell Rev. Jones. (She, like him, seemed quite unaware of the transactions going on at our end.) A moment later Rev. Jones was outside the cubicle. 'Are you trying something on?' he asked, standing discreetly out of view. The irony of his words gave me a pleasure far superior to anything I had so far been offered. 'I think *they're* trying it on,' I answered (the boy had removed his last garment). 'Oh really?' said Rev. Jones. 'Well, don't rush. We're ready when you are. ('Do they need any help?' from Miss Mare. 'I can tell them any relevant vocab.')

Finally we all stumbled out, like characters at the end of a farce, shaking hands and embracing affectionately. The gap-toothed boy raised his fez in salute. The shopkeeper collected our tea-cups on his tray. Our audience of two seemed not to notice us. Miss Mare was admiring the new shoes she had bought. ('He took the broken ones in part-exchange!' she told us with enthusiasm.) 'Were you tempted by anything?' Rev. Jones casually enquired. But before we could reply the 'guide' hustled us out of the shop. His commission not extending to the goods we'd been offered, he was anxious to get rid of us. He took his leave shaking hands in a way that eased the transfer of notes. Rev. Jones coughed up but when my turn came I took only his forefinger. 'That's the way to do it!' Miss Mare said. 'Must remember that one!' I didn't think, after her performance in the shop, she needed any lessons from me.

By now the whole population was climbing up behind the town to the old Spanish barracks where the festival was to take place. Some little girls barked out 'No!' at the sight of G's camera. As so often in religious revivals, the most devout are the very young and female. (Also of course, the children are closest to Koranic School influence and the teachings of traditional Islam.)

Miss Mare was disappointed that the event should be confined to one area. 'Not advisable with this size crowd – look at them all, up in the trees already – difficult to get a good view. Last year they had it all over the hills – thirteen tribes of them at it. Looks like only three this year. Very poor show.'

What the tribes were 'at' was mass gyration of the cliché Hollywood oriental kind: all writhing away while a tinny band with bongo drums played around them, same tune over and over again. The women were most active, putting their all into it. The men more casual; barely going through the motions. 'The men don't seem to be doing much,' I observed to Rev. Jones. 'Well, they never do, do they?' he replied languidly. I was beginning to take to him. Throughout the afternoon he was much more forthcoming about himself, entirely dropping the derelict preacher guise of his church appearances for something altogether racier. Said he'd read Edmund Gosse. Also Hugh Kingsmill. *Lapped* up Evelyn Waugh but found Alec's books 'very hard going' (strange how difficult popular fiction can be). He explained how he'd tried to learn Welsh. But there was no 'j' and for words like 'jam' they just added an 'o' and said 'jammo'. 'I couldn't waste time on a language like that,' he said ruefully.

The religious entertainment soon lost what little appeal it had to begin with. Besides, we decided it was probably unwise to wait till the whole barracks area was filled with the enthusiastic throng. On our way down Miss Mare paused to examine a pile of dismal-looking coins a beggar had strewn beside him on the dusty road. 'I like coins now,' she said gleefully. 'We found a Roman one at Volubilis.' Rev. Jones looked distressed at fresh mention of this topic. Clearly still felt guilty about not handing it in. Even so, to the astonishment of the beggar, he bent down with Miss Mare and in the manner of school chums engaged in a common hobby they rummaged together through the hopeless heap.

Back down towards the sea – cresty white waves thudding round the jetty – we sat outside a café over mint tea (Rev. Jones had a beer). We exchanged notes about our respective tours. Rev. Jones said he thought Rabat a most civilised city and had quite fallen in love with Fez (Miss Mare's name seemed to hang in the air). But he was forced to the conclusion, he said, that it was the hybrid Morocco he took to most. We both agreed. 'I suppose that's why they all say Tangier's un-Moroccan,' he went on. 'But it's just that mixture of Moorish and European that I like.' Miss Mare said Tangier was only un-Moroccan if you had no imagination. True, the medina couldn't be more different from the one at Fez, but in the way two words were different that you could change one into the other a letter at a time. Or the way a composer's first symphony differed from his last. The interest lay in observing the stages, she said, noticing the seeds of the one in the other. 'That's a very good point,' said Rev. Jones.

By now there was quite a festive atmosphere – a kind of Biblical bank holiday. The whole of the little fishing port was alive with activity. Even the hawkers paused only briefly to offer their wares – too busy with celebrations to spend time coaxing customers to buy. But for all the exotic setting and costume I kept thinking of an English crowd at a fairground. Another kind of ritual.

Towards sunset, a movement began back towards the town. People streamed down from the barracks area for the final procession that would lead the dancers to prayer in the sanctuary of the medina. We were perfectly positioned at the end of the route. Soon we could hear the approaching musicians and dancers and the crowd increased. We moved to the roadside and watched the white-clad throng laughing as, tirelessly, they continued the gyrating which had been going on now for the best part of three hours. Shifting forwards at the same time as it danced along, surrounded by spectators, the first 'tribe' came by, preceded by its banner. Everyone jostled beside holding up cassette recorders, taping the proceedings. Behind us G stood on the café table taking photos. As always anxious not to offend he had removed his shoes. The young Moroccans standing on the table laughed; they all wore theirs. They told him he must not think they were interested in these absurd goings-on – which were put on, they said, strictly for the old. Hearing this, I wondered how the Sultan's Islamic revival would fare faced with such indifference among the young: something like sixty per cent of the population is under twenty (and fervent little girls soon grow up into intelligent young women). Those cassette recorders were more than a gross anachronism; they were symbols of the changing culture here.

All at once the other two 'tribes' came rushing down the hill, virtually at the gallop, with a single whistle-blowing policeman before them who made vain efforts to check the pace of their progress. They were all laughing as they streamed along the road pursued by a crowd of young Moroccans. But at the entrance to the medina the leaders suddenly turned back and those behind came to a halt wondering what was happening ahead. Had someone drawn a knife? Panic spread quickly back through the procession and a general flight seemed imminent – with us in the path of escape. For a desperate moment we looked like being at the centre of a religious riot. A group had detached itself and its members pressed up against us, calling in French for us to let them pass on to the pavement. In their sudden state of panic they saw this as the best way out, were perhaps contemplating taking shelter in the café. The only drawback was that we should be crushed to death in the process.

At this critical juncture Miss Mare remained calm. She shook her head resolutely, saying 'No!' repeatedly in French and Arabic. In the face of such total intransigence the crowd lost heart and retreated. The moment of panic passed and the procession moved peacefully into the medina. 'You've got to watch them,' Miss Mare said later. 'Especially in queues. They push in and pick pockets.'

In the twilight – a hazy almost misty one reminiscent of a humid August nightfall in England – we climbed the hill to the car. The festive lights came on. They were lit up here in Tangier too when we got back – but only for an hour: system can't cope with any more. Miss Mare was in a cheerful frame of mind: 'Thought at first it was going to be disappointing, didn't you? But jolly good value in the end.'

Driving back she said suddenly: 'I wonder if the revival of the faith will come from Russia? Certainly won't come from England or America.'

'Or from Wales,' Rev. Jones added.

An odd incident after dinner at the Claridge tonight.

We were sitting on the terrace watching the passing parade when a Pest approached saying, 'Queer men come here for jig-jig with Moroccan boys.' It was nice to hear the word 'jig-jig' with its suggestion of colonial bars and dank Singapore nights. But otherwise there was nothing very remarkable in this statement. Or the Pest who made it. I told him it was extremely true but I myself was sick to death of Moroccan boys, hadn't had jig-jig with a single one of them and would he kindly go away? 'This my country: *you* go!' he retorted and I realised this was another example of babes up in arms. The boy ranted on to the effect that Moroccan males were being exploited and their purity defiled which, after today's goings-on in the carpet shop, one could not listen to with much sympathy. The old Moroccan at the next table said the child was mad. This set the boy off at him for a bit in Arabic, then turning again to us he said vehemently: 'I no take it!' At that moment a middle-aged Moroccan (who earlier had invited us to 'make love tonight, very cheap') passed and hearing the boy's protestation laughed loudly and said: 'Oh yes! He take! He take *very* much!' This was the final straw for the boy who ran off saying he was going to fetch the police. A few minutes later he returned with an older boy on a bike who, putting his arm round him, said he wished to apologise. The boy smiled, bowed and said he was sorry. Coming back here we met him again on the Boulevard. He was with the elderly Englishman we've seen often at the Parade. 'Everything all right now!' he called cheerfully to us. 'Nothing to do – okay?' Then, saying 'See you later, alligator' he went off with the elderly Englishman.

(There is some doubt apparently about the van der Meers keeping on this hotel. This may explain the disappointments of the restaurant. They told us tonight their two sons did not want to stay in Tangier. Esmé: Well, neither of them is gay, you see...)

8 February

8 a.m. On the ferry *Mons Calpe* to Gib. Bacon and egg breakfast at Captain's table: Kellogg's, ketchup, H.P. sauce. Spanish-speaking waiters. All around men in djellabas, women in caftans and veils. One or two lower them as a gesture to leaving Morocco. (Bar full of Brits getting drunk.)

Coming back from Asilah last night, Rev. Jones mentioned the man who made our visit to Fez peculiarly memorable.

Miss Mare had been singing the praises of a Russian Orthodox priest they'd had lunch with in Rabat. (He it must have been who had raised her hopes of a Christian revival in Russia.) Some French woman had insisted the priest was a spy.

'I was furious!' said Miss Mare. 'I really gave it to her. Said, what secrets did she have that he'd want? That shut her up.'

Which brought from Rev. Jones the intriguing remark:

'I always think Harvey Lambert looks like a spy.'

'That's because he's only got one eye,' Miss Mare said.

Later, at the hotel, where we'd invited him for a drink (he accepted with alacrity) Rev. Jones said: 'Did you meet Harvey Lambert at Fez?' I said we had. He was silent a moment. Then: 'Extraordinary man,' he said.

We have not, alas, seen the tall, ambling figure of Harvey Lambert since getting back to Tangier. I'd better take the opportunity of this crossing to Gib – knowing the rarity here of a couple of hours' inactivity – to write up our meeting at Fez, the memory of which will not easily be erased...

On our first evening there we called, as Miss Stray had suggested, at the Hotel Majestic where Harvey Lambert keeps a room. He has a large house in Tangier but teaches English in Fez (Miss Stray: To make ends meet – got family in England).

The hotel was dark and dingy. Porter at the desk very similar. I asked to leave a message. He offered me the phone instead. I thought this intrusive. But porter said Mr Lambert didn't mind. I went ahead.

A slow, aristocratic voice, light but very hesitant. Yes, how nice that we were here. He would consult his diary. Now then, what about – no, that was – or, wait a bit, – but he was returning to Tangier. Oh dear – well—

I said not to worry; we might have the pleasure of seeing him back in Tangier. Oh, but he would like to show us Fez. Look, why not come up now? If we didn't object to pyjamas. I said no, but it was rather late (I had visions of a one-eyed figure in pyjamas ushering us bewildered through a darkened medina). No, no, we wouldn't be disturbing – he was teaching in the morning. Now was the perfect time.

Up we went.

The door of Room One was wide open. Inside a figure, its back to us, stood struggling into a dressing-gown. The adjacent wardrobe mirror reflected a scene of some disorder: every available surface covered with books, newspapers and all manner of odds and ends. An oasis comprising two beds and a chair had been cleared pending our arrival.

We waited outside, hesitating to enter while the figure was enrobing, too far from the open door to knock without being seen, as it were, to be seeing.

At length the figure turned and beckoned to us. We neither of us moved. Miss Stray had prepared us for the lost eye (result of a long distant car crash); but not for the cotton wool covering it.

By the time we'd recovered enough to enter, Lambert was back in bed. G sat on the chair, I had no alternative to the second bed. Seated thus on either side of him, we could not avoid the feel of the hospital visit, which the interview rapidly assumed.

A single fluorescent light illumined the room. To keep its glare off his one eye Lambert drew a green shade across his forehead; otherwise his only reading aid was a gold-rimmed monocle. This, on a ribbon round his neck, he used when quoting from the mass of printed material that surrounded us.

Occasionally he'd pick up a weeks-old Sunday paper and discuss an item from it. But generally the conversation stayed on mythological lines. It was like visiting a retired professor of ancientology now quietly expiring in a hospital bed.

'If you're reading about 6th-century Ireland...' Lambert would begin, as if that were the most likely way we were filling our time. He spoke slowly and in a halting manner; seemed to find the action perplexing. This made for sudden transitions from subject to subject. 'I was reading – where was it?—' (monocle to eye, hand outstretched for book) '—Well – anyway—' (hand retracted, monocle let fall) '—it appears that the death of Osiris was the first recorded instance of tribal panic – hence of course the word—' (G thought this meant the terrified tribe was called 'Panic'; by this stage we were both a bit confused. I suddenly realised that, the lost eye being on my side, Lambert was addressing me through the wardrobe mirror. I found this disconcerting. I didn't, as it were, know where to put my face.)

He talked also of ritual bull-killing in the Atlas Mountains. I said I hoped we were not keeping him up. He said not at all, but perhaps we might meet while we were in Fez (I don't know what he called what we were doing then). He reached for his diary. Tomorrow in the late morning perhaps – or if he *didn't* go back to Tangier – early afternoon was a possibility... Or if he did go back, perhaps we could go with him... Or, should he stay, a mid-evening meet might be on the cards... I thought a drive round the Route du Tour de Fès the best idea. But this – the easiest solution – was the only one he didn't propose.

Finally we invited him to dinner at our hotel. He said that was an excellent idea, but would we like to try a Moroccan restaurant he knew that was rather good? Yes, willingly, we said. That decided, we left barely an hour later...

Next evening, promptly, he arrived at our hotel, the cotton wool (which we'd taken as a night dressing) still in place. Now beneath a broad-brimmed hat. The monocle again hung round his neck over a jet-black cape. 'It's a selham,' he said when I expressed admiration. 'The other day I heard a Western-clad shop-girl say to her friend, "Look at that dog of a Christian in Arab clothes." She didn't know I spoke Arabic. I said, "Your Western clothes don't have Western manners to go with them."'

He laughed in the half-hearted way of someone who has told a poor joke and regrets it. He often laughed like that.

We made to set off but he said on consideration perhaps it was better to dine at our hotel as we'd first suggested. The Moroccan restaurant was some way and the night was chilly.

We should have been relieved at this change of plan. This was the day of our disastrous cous-cous beneath the banana trees, so another suspect – and wineless – meal was not a thing we were looking forward to. But just because of that we'd taken the precaution of eating in advance. Now, to the astonishment of the waiters, we re-entered the hotel dining room. Was there no limit to these European appetites, they must have been thinking as we sat down again. No wonder half the world was starving if this was how the other half lived.

At least first time round we'd ordered just crêpes with a bottle of red wine and some fruit to follow. Even so, neither of us managed to finish the minestrone with which the standard three-course meal began. And by the time a tagine of lamb was set before us, we weren't even managing to start.

'Delicious!' we said, taking tentative dips with the fork while with the knife we crammed the leftovers on one side, trying to disguise the fact that they comprised the whole dish. Lambert said nothing, but even he can't have thought it anything but strange that two people should invite him to dinner who seemed to be on starvation diet.

'What's the wine like?' he asked, clearly surprised that we had scarcely touched the excellent Cabernet to which he'd treated us. 'Excellent!' we chorused, raising our glasses in a sip.

To our horror he'd turned out to be teetotaller (secret convert to Islam?) which left us to demolish the bottle between us. Not a thing that would have troubled us normally. But with so staid and abstemious a guest we felt some obligation to stay reasonably sober; which this second bottle was guaranteed to prevent.

All the same, we could hardly leave so good a wine; while coming clean meant revealing the doubts over Lambert's choice of restaurant that had prompted our behaviour but which it would scarcely be courteous to relate. Hoist by our own petard, we could only sit watching the wine disappear down the bottle like an hour-glass measuring the sands of our sobriety.

As if divining the need to avoid all sleep-inducing topics, Lambert kept the conversation off mythology. Somehow we survived the meal relatively unscathed (though the waiters, whether from a simple desire to please or an attempt to punish our apparent gluttony it wasn't clear, pressed on us every available item).

But over coffee in the lounge ('*Do* have a cognac!') things soon took a recondite course. Lambert began harmlessly enough by relating how staying the extra day in Fez on our account had brought an offer he would otherwise have missed. (This made him all the more generous towards us: 'Have some whiskey – just to finish!' he insisted.) It seemed some friends of his had called saying he could rent the penthouse they were buying: making life considerably more civilised than in Room One at the Majestic. These friends happening to be a Russian prince and princess, the talk turned naturally to the Romanov dynasty. Lambert was quite an expert on the Romanov dynasty, especially on the Anastasia question. He talked a lot about the Anastasia question. Sleep irresistibly began to beckon.

Even without the alcohol I should probably have been in trouble: for me, genealogy has always been a potent anaesthetic. With it, mere mention of the word was enough to send me off.

For a while G held the fort. But he too was fading fast. (At one point we both nodded off together.) Lambert rambled on regardless; seemed completely unperturbed. Perhaps his one eye meant he couldn't see the scale of our collapse. Or maybe he was used to inattention (he was a teacher after all). Sometimes in my comatose condition I sensed that I was seeing through the years back to the schoolboy Lambert: not a swot – his interests too far off the beaten track for that; but 'inky', always deep in broody books, already rarefied, made fun of. Happier to be ignored.

I kept dozing, waking every now and then with a terrifying jerk that made me think my neck was broken. In between, vague names and phrases floated in, like scraps of jetsam on the shore: the Archimandrite of Tchudov... 'The Turkish Intermezzo'... Count Brümmer... Leopold of Mecklenburg...

'Really? I didn't know that,' I would drone; 'how bor— *interest*ing, I mean.'

By now my view of everything was, to say the least, impressionistic. Yet I gained insights I might not have done sober. (How appropriate that I should see essential truths about life here in an alcoholic stupor.)

For those half-heard fragments of Lambert's – about Russian exiles and whatever – prompted my subconscious to fling up flotsam of its own: memories of the London language schools where malign fate had from time to time consigned me. I thought of the upper-class drop-outs and good-family-failures of which those places are full: debris of a system in decay, cast out to drift among the shallows of a still unformed successor, salvaging some vestiges of prestige from native (if imperfect) knowledge of a language all the world now wants to learn.

Suddenly I saw Lambert – and all the Tangier people – as part of that twilight world. For the language school inmates are exiles of a kind themselves: internal exiles, as it were, in retreat from modern life and a system to which they are either opposed or at least unsympathetic. Not at all a bad thing in itself; except when accompanied, as in their case it is, by promotion of a Britain long since vanished but easy to believe in if you spend your time with foreigners whose preconceived views it confirms.

But however successful this self-deception, it leads inescapably to the predicament of all exiles – whether social, political, intellectual, or simply financial; seekers after romance as much as those just in search of a standard of living no longer possible at home: the restless sensation of being cast adrift from one world, never anchored in another. That is unmistakably the fate of people here. But it took that bizarre meeting with Harvey Lambert in Fez to alert me to the parallel with Britain which suggests it might be our fate there as well.

7 p.m. Now writing on the boat *back* from Gib. Much more crowded than coming over. On deck despite chill breeze. (Bar full of Brits getting drunk.)

I think I am suffering from culture lag. Yesterday we were in Asilah watching religious rites being recorded by spectators on cassettes. A day or two before we were in a fully functioning mediaeval city dining with a man whose terms of reference make the mediaeval seem almost contemporary. Now we are returning from a place where the time scale appeared no less remote and the cultural mix if anything more grotesque still.

In retrospect, that evening in Fez with Lambert has the quality of a dream. What were we doing there, at that time, in that place, with that extraordinary person? How had we, with our differing backgrounds, come upon him with his? Who ordained this event in life's itinerary? (...*and then on Thursday the 31st January 197– you have dinner with a Mr Harvey Lambert in Fez...*)

I have a similar sense of unreality now (I even wrote Harvey *Fez* in that last sentence). We are on the Tangier ferry crossing the Straits of Gibraltar (and the muezzin is calling the faithful on board to prayer). Seems an odd place to be on a Friday evening in February. Emerging into the sunshine from the tea-shop in Gib you could imagine you were in the Home Counties on a summer afternoon circa 1960 about to drive back to London. And the sound of Spanish alternating with fluent, idiomatic English, suggested more the mid-point between the Americas than the division of Europe and Africa. (On the deck here a dozen djellaba-clad figures have answered the call and are prostrating themselves due east.)

Yet to all these people this ferry is as much part of their everyday life as a number twelve bus is to me. Throughout the globe other boats are plying back and forth in the same nondescript way, to everyone on them making a journey that is an ordinary event. All that activity going on day in, day out. Immersed in your own world, you barely acknowledge the existence of others.

(We are coming into Tangier. As a Sultan returning from Europe once put it: good to be back in civilisation.)

9 February

The disembarkation was a nightmare. Absolute chaos. All the Moroccans returning from their week's work on the Rock (where they've replaced the Spanish since the closing of the border). Over an hour before we could get off. Retreated from the fray. Read Conrad's *Chance*. Luckily our taxi from the morning turned up as we'd asked, so we could escape from all the others who besieged us the moment we were off the boat.

Not that it had been any easier on the Gib side. Huge passport queues. All the horrors of British officialdom and the refugee squalor of the Channel ports.

There was much to remind one of home in Gib: high prices, poor value, the odd vandalised phone box. (Bars full of Brits getting drunk.) The Rock Hotel has that plush plastic look one knows so well and the service that quintessentially British air of resentment. In the harsh Spanish light (compared with this soft Tangier kind) we climbed to a restaurant called 'Le Jardin': 'set in a lovely garden scenery' (Gib brochure). A swarthy proprietor greeted us, took us into a dark, cheerless interior. At the mention of 'garden' pointed to a few wilting plants.

We stormed out, as in England, muttering about trades descriptions. Had lunch in a café in the park. Self-service, slop-tray, revolting sandwiches. Old incomprehensible crone at the counter. Ask for wine. She waves a dusty, vinegary-looking bottle that could well have survived one of the sieges. Have stale rolls and beer. Part with many pounds.

But besides these familiar hallmarks of Britain Present, there was much evidence of Britain Past. John Bull jollity, full-blooded but somehow suggesting there isn't really much to be glad about. Policemen directing traffic for want of other occupation. Condensed milk in tea; Tiger bread toast; hideous cakes of a kind I'd not seen since childhood: fragments of our national heritage rare in these days of wine bars and bistros. And presented with that passion for awfulness for which Britain was once famous. Each horrible item laid lovingly before you, in the firm conviction you were bound to enjoy it. In the tea-shop no ghastly extra was too much trouble: 'More margarine? Another marzipan wafer? Vinegar with your tinned sardines?'

This catering nightmare of the past peacefully co-exists in Gib with the latter-day version which loses nothing in shoddiness but swaps courtesy for schadenfreude. For the expatriate Tangieros here, Gib must constitute the worst of both worlds: the Britain they fled from and the one they've no wish to return to.

We went to the top of the Rock in the cable car. Operator cracked bar-room jokes all the way in Birmingham accent and wartime slang. Views of Malaga along the coast, Algeciras across the bay, Morocco across the straits. We could see both the closed Spanish frontier and Spain's Moroccan Gibraltar: Ceuta – never mentioned when the future of the Rock is debated.

For all that, up there the Spanish point of view made more sense. Far below us the Mediterranean shimmered and sparkled like silk in the brilliant sunshine, serene yet full of movement, seeming little to do with Britain. Even here the Latin strain in the British temper remained bottled up: no outdoor cafés, no concession to sun and sea. Gibraltar is a cross between Dorset and Dieppe: no further south than that. While Britain has taken to itself the pleasures of France and Italy and Spain it used to disdain but has now discovered en masse (thus destroying the myth of foreign inferiority), Gibraltar preserves the remnants of the old Imperial approach: Britain is Britain wherever it may be; abroad is abroad. It's one thing to *import* a foreign influence, when it counts almost as plunder and can satisfy the sense of romance; quite another to be seen succumbing to it on the spot. You could build tropical gardens in Scotland; an Italianate village in Wales; Palladian terraces in England. Or act plays out of doors in the rain, hold garden parties in gales, go to all lengths to bring the South nearer or pretend to be nearer the South. *In* the South, though, you held back. Recreated Guildford or Dorking. Built another Lyme Regis. Sat stubbornly eating indoors.

So Gib's Alameda Gardens were exactly the hybrid kind you'd expect to find at home in one of those attempts at transplanting the South: Mediterranean exuberance carefully tempered by English cool. The local influence was absorbed but the presence of the imperial power still asserted. I thought how Britain itself was a similar hybrid now, the version of itself you'd expect to find artificially produced in America: Ye Olde Englande of Yore but given all the American mod cons (*without-which-civilisation-as-we-know-it-would-cease-to-exist*). Matthew Arnold's 'Anglo-Saxon contagion', I suppose. Coming, as he predicted, from across the Atlantic rather than Britain itself, and now rebounding on the mother country. Classic case of child ingratitude (parental revenge?). Greece and Rome over again.

On the way back to the boat, wandered round the Trafalgar Cemetery. Pretty triangular graveyard for the wounded of the battle who subsequently died (those killed outright being buried at sea). With the blue sky, warm sunshine, scent of flowers and birds singing, like an English country churchyard on a fine day of summer. But the nostalgia of the place overshadowed by its sadness. Lives wasted in victories now meaningless, and all the arrogance, stubbornness and notions of superiority that went into them and brought glory now the source of the intransigence that brings only isolation. Britain looks to Europe in the same half-hearted way Morocco does to Islam.

We saw Harvey Lambert in the street today. Approached from behind. He rounded on us as if expecting attack. (Had I been an assailant that cotton wool would've stopped me in my tracks.) Seemed embarrassed when he saw who it was. Said: 'Rather nervous, I'm afraid.' Instantly took out his diary. 'Mid-evening tomorrow… or else perhaps late afternoon the day after…' But we couldn't find a suitable time. He looked crestfallen. Said: 'Even so, we really must…'

(An invitation has finally arrived from Tommy Bidfine. He asks us to Nettlewood – for tea…)

10 February

G has dutifully gone to church. I couldn't face it. Said I'd join him for the social afterwards.

Rang Bidfine to confirm, incidentally asking for the Tangier directory and being given a single volume for the whole of Morocco.

On the phone, Bidfine sounded peeved. Apparently he'd rung twice while we were away. I said I was sorry we'd missed him. But there was no shortage of opportunities before that: we saw him early on at the Brigadier's, and two or three times in the street after that. Always he'd extended an invitation without fixing a date (the exact opposite of Harvey Lambert whose diary is seldom out of his hand but too full to be of use). Clearly Château Bidfine has a carefully worked out system of admissions:

1. *First Meeting* (preliminary contact)
2. *Subsequent Encounters* (tentative invites)
3. *Final Summons.*

But the scheme backfired with us because by the time we reached the qualifying round we weren't here.

Anyhow, Bidfine was most concerned to emphasise he lived on the *Old* Mountain. He gave the word a special quavering stress: '*Vieille* Montagne, *Vecchio* Montagno, any language you please. My house is Nettlewood, *Old* Mountain. Tell the taxi driver to stop at the sanctuary of Sidi Shiftay – as in the late lamented Rev. Shiftey.' He laughed briefly then went on that if we did not follow his directions to the letter we should be taken to the *New* Mountain, which he obviously considered a world wholly different from his.

12 February

The taxi driver was receptive to Bidfine's instructions. After crossing a poor outlying suburb (where one of the waiters from the hotel seeing us smiled and waved till we were out of sight), we came, in sudden contrast, to an exquisite winding lane, climbing steeply uphill, like a country lane in England. All along it stood the old mossy walls of houses set among lush vegetation. Finally we stopped outside a big gate and an old-fashioned bell-pull. Long pause after we'd rung it. Then a small head peered over the wall. A little black-haired girl. She opened the gate. Disappeared. We ambled in – into a rambling, overgrown garden sweeping magnificently downhill. Birds twittering, sweet smell of flowers in the humid afternoon air. Before us, the house. Before it, the view – which even by the standards of 'The View' was overwhelming. We stood dazedly looking at it. Then dazedly rang the doorbell. Some time passed (the siesta habit is ingrained in everyone here). No problem occupying ourselves though. We stared and stared at that view.

Finally Bidfine appeared, dressed with old-fashioned casualness – cavalry twills, retaining like most people the fashions of their youth – come from the afternoon nap that makes up for his insomniac nights. At once he led us down through the garden. 'You see,' he began, 'you thought I was white trash, didn't you? But look! – my land extends right down to those distant palms, as far as the eye can see – be careful, you're treading on fuscias and, oh dear, you've scared away the guinea fowl. *fuchsias*

'But have you ever seen a better view than this? You see the Atlantic; and the Straits; and Spain; and Gibraltar; and Jbel Moussa. On a clear day you even see Portugal. You see everything in fact. But you *don't* see Tangier. That is the advantage of the *Old* Mountain. You are completely hidden from sight of all modern unpleasantness. And that is why I live here. There are a dozen or so villas on the Old Mountain and they all belong to Continental people who come here two weeks a year. Except for me. I alone am here all the time.'

This is no exaggeration of the aggressively defensive style of speech Bidfine from the outset adopted; as if he knew everything that was being said about him – or thought was – and wanted to forestall all possible criticism with a disarming remark for each hypothetical charge. The 'white trash' reference bewildered me. He seemed to be saying he wasn't just some run-to-seed nobody but the owner of the best villa in Tangier with the best garden and best view (and not just some absentee owner either). Well, this was simply British chauvinism in little; nothing remarkable about that. In Britain everything British is always best and Bidfine being British, there was no reason why he shouldn't adopt the same stance regarding himself. But 'white trash' was an unfortunate choice of expression, having acquired from the days of Hippiedom the sense of a rich white with all the trappings of luxury – a description that would fit Bidfine exactly were it not for just the romantic run-down grandeur of Nettlewood he seemed so anxious to renounce. Throughout our visit I noticed contradictions of this kind.

We went inside the house, a classic very beautiful Colonial-style villa of the early 19th century, to which two neo-Gothic wings have been attached. Everything within is plain and simple, antique only in the sense of having been long in use. Not at all 'done up' – he had confined himself to major repairs: the walls undecorated, except by pictures; the furniture sparse and elegant.

In the study, a ceiling of lovely wooden boards. Of heating, small sign beyond oil stoves. The floors bare except in the bathroom which is covered in beautiful blue and green triangular tiles. 'Moorish,' said Bidfine, 'but brought from my house in Spain. I replaced them there with modern bathroom tiles which impressed the vulgar people who bought it enough for the agent to raise the price. D'you like my cistern? It's called "The Real Niagara".'

During this tour of the building, Bidfine again occasionally spoiled the effect by pointing something out with similar self-conscious remarks which would have been in keeping with the kind of person he neither was nor clearly wished to be thought: 'Not very old – 1810 or so,' he commented in a blasé way of a piece one of us had admired. And in general: 'Yes, we have all mod cons, yet everything otherwise is authentic – as such a house would always have been.' So of course it was; but unnecessary to say so. But this is often the case when you are on the shy side and meeting someone for the first time; in the process you give a bad impression of yourself.

As a result, Bidfine must have spoken for all but a few minutes of the initial hour's conversation – constantly apologising for talking about himself before still going on to do so. Nervousness deriving probably from lack of charm of which he is aware, being a big, broad man with grey-white hair and a prominent nose that upsets otherwise good features. A painting on the wall shows him as a blond, distinguished- (rather than good-) looking young man of the old aristocratic type. The picture reminded G of Anthony Blunt. I thought of the young Auden. A face full of hauteur, of the old English breed. But the 'rarllys' (for 'really') and 'chars' (for 'chair') seemed a little suspect to my ear. Perhaps all I'm saying is that Bidfine could be a Wykehamist. Or was in the Guards.

Points revealed during the monologue:

Quite unable to tolerate England after the war – the usual refrain here. Esmé said: 'I stayed on a year or two. Couldn't stand it.' And Alec Waugh referred to not being able to get a suit. 'You've no idea what it was like,' Bidfine now said. They all make the mistake of thinking this, because they regard the young in a variation of the way the young are thought to regard the old: just as for the young the old scarcely exist in the present, so for these people the young have not existed in the past. But I was a child in the post-war period and have a child's vivid memories of it: of rationing which in our dismal part of London made us concerned more about where the next meal rather than suit would come from; of queuing in the cold for, of all things, orange juice whose metallic taste I detested.

I was inclined to mention these things to Bidfine, but refrained. It's as boring to go on about your poverty as it is to bewail your richesse. So I was amused when Bidfine was himself reduced to these tactics by a phone call that interrupted us at this point: 'Dotty, my dear! How *are* you? What? …Well, I rather think, my dear, that most people instead of worrying about where to get chauffeurs are anxious to hang on to their *fatima*…' Bidfine himself has no servant problem, though, as will appear.

He'd lived in Spain for some dozen years. But grew tired of it 'when things got worse'. (I thought he was referring to Franco, but he meant the influx of touristos on the south coast where he lived.) 'So I considered my priorities – everyone has priorities, the things they can't do without. Mine were: servants – I've never had any idea what goes on in the kitchen, all matters of practicality are beyond me. So servants were number one. Number two: a pleasant climate. Number three: intelligent compatriots to talk to in one's native lingo. Number four: reasonable proximity to England. Well, it was too late for Jamaica – too far anyway; but everyone was already coming back from there. *Most* unpleasant.' (I recalled something on this from both Esmé and the Waughs, who'd had Jamaican interludes). 'Then I chanced to come to Tangier – to see an old friend. The place immediately appealed to me, and seemed to satisfy my four requirements. I went to house agents, started looking at properties. Found nothing to my taste. Till one day I was walking here on the Mountain and peeped over this wall. I knew straightaway this was it!'

By now we were seated in the study – with that view before us – and at this moment a lean and serene Moroccan came silently in with the tea tray. He deposited it, stood eyes lowered for a second, then inclining his head backed out of the room.

'Thank you, Mustafa,' said Bidfine. He moved to pour the tea from the silver pot. 'Mustafa is the perfect servant. So is his wife. So are all my servants. Oh, I know all about the Hubert-Smythes with their liveried butler and all the rest—' (the Hubert-Smythes! My ears pricked up at this name but I missed the chance to pursue the subject) '—but they all go home and watch TV in the evenings,' Bidfine continued. 'Whereas this is the only house that has *resident* servants. You remember Mr Pepys—' (he pronounced it 'Pèpiz': 'that's how they said it') '—and how he referred to "my family" – he included his servants. Well, I'm the same.' He pointed to a large photograph on the wall of a group seated in front of the house. Bidfine sat resplendent in a white tropical suit at the centre, a young man and woman on either side of him, the faithful servants – including Mustafa and his wife – standing behind. 'My nephew's wedding,' said Bidfine. 'We held the reception here. You see, this is *my* family!' (Even so, he had cut off the front of the house from the back which has become 'the servants' quarters: servants, like climates and children, should know their place and not inconvenience one'.)

'Now where was I? Ah yes. How I came by Nettlewood. Well, cunningly, I sought out the owner – always cut out the middleman. He was someone with the marvellously Wodehousian name of the Hon. Lauderdale Montmorency-Mount – a relative of the Marquess of Henley – also of our own dear Hon. – Anthony

Crashaw here whom you may have met.' (He was the wizened elderly man we saw with Brandon Brendon/Brendon Brandon at the restaurant with the Waughs.) 'Well, the house had been theirs for years – now virtually derelict with a couple of missionaries or whatever living in it.' (Bidfine described these as 'squatters', a rare intrusion of the modern world into his vocabulary.)

'So. I considered what I had, and what I would have,' he went on, '– you know: one's income comes in – and made the highest offer I could. Of course, after independence here property prices went down but by this time they were creeping up again. Mr Mount came to Tangier to talk – though naturally money was never mentioned. He was really just vetting me. Negotiations went through the agent. So we met and had a very nice dinner – at your hotel (where the food, alas, is now indifferent: they lost their cook). And of course with all the courtesy and generosity for which the British aristocracy is renowned, he turned me down.'

Bidfine screwed up his face in a smile meant to be urbane but that came out evil. '*Do* help yourselves to more cake. Mustafa's wife got it specially.'

It was with typical understatement that he mentioned only the cake. Before us was brown bread-and-butter, immaculate cucumber sandwiches, toasted muffins, honey and apricot jam. The old nursery tea (almost unobtainable now at home) perfectly transplanted to Morocco. Bidfine beamed proudly at the spread. 'It's just like the England of old here, isn't it? The England we all knew and loved. Well, some of us.'

He waited till we pressed him before continuing ('You're sure I'm not boring you?'):

'Oh yes – well, a little time passed and then – a thing out of Dickens: I had a windfall! Elderly relative died – you won't believe it! – left me *everything*. I *rarlly* expected the police round any day! So, I found I could raise my offer. I wrote again to Mr Mount. He kept me waiting two weeks. Then accepted. So here I am, have been, and ever shall be! Absurd offers are made for houses here – half a million and whatever. But Nettlewood... is not for sale.'

As he concluded this account of his coming (on a note of finality that had in it a distinct touch of doom, I thought) Mustafa reappeared carrying a silver-plated kettle of hot water. Silently he approached the teapot, decorously removed its lid, replenished it, then retreated, as before backwards, out of the room.

'Thank you, Mustafa,' said Bidfine. Then: 'Is that your bag resting against my lovely vase? Will you take it away please?'

Bidfine spoke sharply, addressing G.

'No, it's mine,' I said, removing the offending bag. 'Where did you get it?' I asked of the lovely vase, trying to cover my embarrassment at my host's solecism.

'John dear,' Bidfine began, reverting to his urbane manner but with a touch of the Mustafa idiom; then recounted the well-known story of Edward Lear and Queen Victoria that ends with the Queen's reproving remark: 'Mr Lear, I inherited it!'

I smiled (I'd heard it many times). 'I suppose I might just pass for Edward Lear,' I said lightly, 'but I find it hard to see you as the Queen, Tommy.' (The rapier I reserve for self-defence.)

An odd interruption occurred at this point. The little girl whose head had appeared over the wall on our arrival, now entered and signified without speaking that a visitor was at the gate.

'Admit him,' said Bidfine.

The girl left and Bidfine said: 'Who can this be? I was expecting no one but yourselves.'

The girl returned to indicate that the visitor was now at the door. Bidfine excused himself and went out. We heard a cry of recognition as he caught sight of his visitor, then the sounds of an exchange between them, conducted on the visitor's side in the low tone of someone begging a favour. Then Bidfine returned to the room, went to his desk, lifted his monocle to his eye and swiftly wrote out a cheque. This he took with him to the front door. The visitor spoke again but in the louder, more confident tone of success. 'Thank you. Most grateful. Very good of you. Have to go to Gib you see. Otherwise wouldn't trouble you...' Remarks Bidfine punctuated with 'Quites', 'Not at alls' and 'Of courses'. But unmistakably the voice of the visitor was Harvey Lambert's.

'Money is such a sordid business!' Bidfine said, coming in again. He refilled the tea-cups. 'Alas, it is essential for freedom.'

The conversation continued along these lines for a few minutes and G said it was dangerous to attach too much importance to money; people who did so inevitably suffered for it and became miserable. This became one of G's endearing dropped bricks, since making money turned out to be the cornerstone of Bidfine's philosophy.

'I disagree with you,' he said, gently but firmly. 'The way to independence is to make money. It is quite impossible otherwise. I can't emphasise enough how essential it is. Without it, we shouldn't be sitting here at Nettlewood cosily drinking tea together from this charming bone china.'

He had been unforthcoming about his background in England, vaguely referring to being educated 'at university there, for a very short time'. Now, without furnishing further details, he explained how at eighteen he had set out to make money. And succeeded.

'It's easy to make money. It always is. I could do the same today. I'd become a dustman if there was no alternative. Dustmen earn lots of money and get lots of perks. They make special deals with hotels to visit two or three times a week, for a special fee. I'd soon have enough to invest. And I'd invest wisely, as I always have. Of course, you must live in one place and have your money elsewhere. Which means leaving England – people pay tax there. But then leaving England is no hardship. It has very little to recommend it, England. I couldn't live there. I go there once or twice a year to see friends and people.' He paused a moment, then said with sudden intensity: 'But I hate England.' He paused again, then perhaps because one of us had smiled as if he were joking, repeated: 'I really do' (losing, in the desire to be serious about it, his old-world pronunciation of 'really').

'I hate it,' he said again, with even greater force, and the vehemence with which he spoke made me think there must be some undisclosed aspect of his life there which rankled. Impossible to pursue of course; in any case I was more interested in speculating on the wider mystery behind a man whose performance was so fixed and thoroughly worked out. Public figures such as Jo Grimond and Edward Heath came to mind as well as one or two people of similar generation and background I knew personally: a witty journalist who'd also set out to make money (and, though ending up impoverished, had a serenity I'd not yet observed in Tommy Bidfine); and an industrial executive whose extreme urbanity cloaked an inner sense of failure born of too great a respect for convention. I drew on my knowledge of these to explain the things about Bidfine that puzzled me. I even thought of one or two of my contemporaries Bidfine put me in mind of: his clipped manner when being funny, or (at his best) outrageous, recalling one; his habit of accompanying tags like 'Ah, is it so?' with a wistful look, eyes raised to heaven, making me think of another. But despite all these deliberations I'd so far drawn a blank.

Bidfine may have detected my curiosity because he now tried to pass off his remarks about England in a more light-hearted way: 'I mean, what can you think of a supposedly great city like London where you can't even get monocle cord? *Rar*lly!' he went on, feigning indignation at our laughter but secretly pleased that we had risen to his distracting bait; 'I had to go to Paris, where I'm happy to say I bought the entire stock of the one shop that sold it and have consequently cornered the European market! As I've done with so many things!'

By now the light was beginning to fade and we settled down to watch darkness fall over that incomparable view.

'Make yourselves comfortable,' said Bidfine, 'for we are going to enjoy a magnificent spectacle, the kind of command performance for which Nettlewood is renowned. This is the finest place from which to observe the celebrated Tangier twilight. I have visited most parts of our globe but know nowhere that rivals it. There is something about the quality of the twilight here that, once you have experienced it, captivates you for ever. We all succumb to it. People excuse themselves on account of it, hating to miss it. Yes, sunset is the most important event of the day in Tangier. But not only because of its aesthetic beauty,' he added, and now his voice changed, acquiring a tone of sympathy not at all sincere but seductive for that very reason: it conveyed a sublime resignation to his own superiority that was not just likeable but inspired active admiration, as if love of truth alone compelled him to recognise what otherwise he would only with the utmost reluctance acknowledge. 'Have you noticed,' he asked in this tone, 'how people here always say they must be off, they have lots to do and so on? Well, of course they have *nothing* to do! That is why, even if sunset here were anything less than the wonderful phenomenon it is, they would still be glad when it came. Because it means another uneventful day has passed uneventfully, the important thing being that it has passed. For me, however,' he continued as the wonderful phenomenon began, 'all this is a background to what I came here to accomplish. When I came here, I resolved not to play bridge or watch television. Four nights a week people play here! I couldn't fritter away time like that! No!' he concluded, his expression glazed now in the glow from the spectacle before us. *'These are important years…'*

As he ran us back ('You being such charming guests I am actually going into town after dark. Now how's that?') Bidfine said: 'The delightful thing about life up here is that it has nothing to do with Morocco, nothing to do with Africa, nothing for that matter to do with the whole world!'

22 February

It's taken me a week to start writing again – encouraged by the first glow of light (sunshine is too strong a word) since we got back.

The flight was a swift journey from summer to winter. Over Africa and Spain, the sun was so strong and clear that every detail could be made out below. A few patches of cloud clung to the mountains – but white, summery cloud. Not till western France did we meet that northern cloud, the uniform blanket kind, like a bare wall of concrete, lacking all definition.

There was a taxi strike the day we left. It began at two o'clock. At half past I asked the receptionist how we could get to the airport. He said he would ring for a taxi. I said the taxis were on strike. He said the strike was over. 'We lose interest very quickly,' he explained. 'At first we are enthusiastic. Then a fatalistic lethargy overcomes us.' I said the English were similar. We called it moderation.

At the airport, despite tight security, we managed to get through without boarding cards. The official on the runway horrified. Sent us back as the plane was revving. My spirits rose (a week till the next one!). 'Mais vous partirez!' he assured us. Spirits return to base.

We descended to London as through smog, down into a grimy landscape shut off from all light. Briefly you knew how it felt to be losing your sight. Everything monochrome and indistinct, drained of colour and vitality, with the subdued look of a place newly conquered. A world in twilight, but not the magical Tangier kind. Perhaps I've succumbed to it myself.

(A letter awaited us from the Bank Manager: 'Are there funds in the pipeline?')

23 February

Today has been bright and balmy. But Tangier still seems very remote. I really *miss* those people: Esmé and Bidfine (Nettlewood I can't believe exists); the Waughs; the Brigadier; Miss Stray; the Spicers even (whom we didn't see latterly: but I still hear the manic laughter of that lunch). And I brood on the mystery of the Hubert-Smythes' politics. (Ironically, they got back from Paris the day we were leaving.) And on the extraordinary Harvey Lambert.

A day or two before we left we were lunching on the terrace when suddenly the head waiter – a Grand Vizier type of figure – came round the corner of the building at a rate of knots (bizarre for a Moroccan), with what looked like an inspector of police (school of Agatha Christie) in train. Final sequence in some old Scotland Yard movie. Coming in for the kill. With us as the target.

Of course, it was Harvey Lambert, bringing us a package to take back. On it he'd inscribed the words: Not Needed Till Voyage Has Begun. My mind raced: elegant liner – dinner at Captain's Table – bets on the day's run… (Also Rev. Jones' suspicions of Lambert as spy.)

Lambert hovered as usual, fingered his diary (but even he saw its futility at that stage). 'Don't disturb yourselves,' he said as I rose to offer him my seat. Then launched a few inconsequential snippets:

– The view from this hotel hasn't changed in a hundred years…
– My mother stayed here in 1901…
– That big tree is a sastuzza. Produces a flower like a bird…

A few more and he was gone, leaving me with the impression of having been in a cross between *Night in Casablanca* and *Kind Hearts and Coronets*.

On our last day we treated Miss Stray to martinis at Porte's. She sat sipping contentedly, the plumbing in rare working order. But when we presented her with the bottle of gin we'd brought back from Gib, the cistern flushed close to bursting. 'I'll be the most popular gal in Tangier!' she said, and offered her cheek to be kissed.

We strolled afterwards along the Boulevard, Miss Stray walking at her slow, stately pace, swaying gently from side to side, a distinctive figure in her green turban, long earrings dangling from her head, large handbag from her arm: Wraf and raffish the only way to describe it. She addressed passing acquaintances in Spanish, muttered words of Arabic at Moroccans, gossiped all the way in English to us. In the Rue de la Liberté, she began to wax lyrical about the Porte's cheese biscuits. 'They're frightfully expensive. Forty dirhams a kilo.' We took the hint and she bundled us into the shop that sells them (which we happened to be passing). 'You can buy them by the hundred grams,' she said tactfully. We bought her half a kilo, the same for ourselves. (As we came out, she remarked to the Spanish proprietess: 'Friends of mine. I'll be in again,' and winked. The native habits are catching.)

The others we said goodbye to only briefly (except Bidfine and those at Nina's lunch – of which more anon): outside the church the Sunday before we left. Rev. Jones looked transformed by the engagement. Or at least by the prospect of Tangier retirement (which can never have been high on his options in Wales). Miss Mare was also buoyant. She wore a new flat hat. The Hon. Anthony Crashaw shook my hand. (A girl at the hotel said he was mad but to me he seemed quite unremarkable.) At that final Sunday congregation we met the British Consul-General. He looked very foreign. He was just back from leave and offered to show us over the Consulate. On our last morning we arrived and signed our names in the Visitors' Book, using the ball-point quill provided. The building dates from 1890 when it served as the Ministerial residence (the consulate being then in the medina). After our tour with the Consul we wandered through the gardens, and back to the gates where the porter saluted us. His fez bore the royal arms. As we strolled away we stopped for a final look at the building, very white and colonial in the bright sunshine. At that moment Alec Waugh was slowly approaching it, looking in his loud check jacket so astonishingly like his brother that I laughed out loud at the grotesque idea of Evelyn being retired in Tangier. We waved, but he didn't see us. He had turned in at the gates and our last glimpse of him was as he entered the Consulate Library, stick in one hand, books in the other.

7 p.m.
The Gib ferry will be returning to Tangier.

Two months ago the last thing to occur to me at seven o'clock on a Saturday would've been the Gib ferry. Now I sit here pathetically drinking tea from the Moorish teapot we brought back (sole souvenir), playing those Beethoven sonatas (which for me have acquired associations the composer can never have intended), pining for the romance, the endless picturesqueness, of Tangier, of Morocco.

On our last evening we watched the sunset from the gardens of the former Mendoub's House (*Mediterranean Winter Resorts*: Particularly fine *in twilight*). The house had often been mentioned to us as Forbes' Palace – after its American millionaire owner. Forbes gives extravagant parties and collects toy soldiers. Though it was past closing-time we were allowed to see the collection (our ploy for gaining admission).

The custodian ushered us into the hall where eight motorbikes were parked. A little insignificant man scampered across and wheeled one away, averting his eyes from our gaze. 'Evening, Mr Forbes,' said the custodian.

We passed through roomfuls of glass cases. 'There are forty thousand exhibits here,' said the custodian. I got the impression visitors were fewer. We combined maximum show of interest with minimum inspection, all the time hurrying towards the real object of our visit.

Outside in the terraced gardens the spectacle had begun. With the long façade of the house between us and 'The View' before us, we roamed happily in that blue-pink gloaming. Not till it was completely dark would we allow the custodian to let us out.

Yesterday, I watched the sunset over Hampstead. Wasn't the same. The sunset was attractive in its own way. But Hampstead wasn't the same. Picturesqueness now has scarcity value here. Only a few can afford it. For the rest it's accessible as the paintings in the National Gallery are: always on hand and viewable without charge, but no longer part of life. Carefully conserved just because it's not. Bearing as much relation to the world now as those toy soldiers of Forbes' to a real army; and like them enshrined in showcases. On the way back to the Tube, I almost looked for the custodian to let me out. When I say I'm pining for the romance of Tangier, of Morocco, it's really the romance of England, of Britain I'm missing. I feel almost like an exile here myself. Without having left the country.

24 February

Sunday. A *super*-Sunday. A nadir-grey day. What Esmé St Clair called 'perfect suicide weather'. How remote that lunch seems that he and Nina gave us at the Février villa! It was the day after our visit to Nettlewood and the New Mountain did suggest the wholly different world Bidfine considered it. Had none of the decaying, almost sinister romance of the winding lane to Nettlewood. And the Villa Février had about it a freshness that was quite absent the day we'd had tea there with Nina and Esmé, and Mrs Février appeared. This time a feeling of enormous relief hung in the air, as though a heavy dominating presence had been removed. Which I suppose it had.

The house looked magnificent in the brilliant sunshine. The view – albeit of Tangier and the 'modern world' banished from Nettlewood – much clearer than on our first visit. Esmé welcomed us, looking ill and full of self-loathing. Amusing though. There was quite a sense of occasion. G took photos of everyone as we sat on the terrace over lengthy drinks – there'd been a major setback in the kitchen. Esmé had had to improvise a coq au vin, having discovered the meat for his bœuf bourgignon was hopelessly tough. 'We sent the chauffeur for it and he brought back totally unsuitable stuff.' I said the meat varied a lot in Tangier. 'No,' said Esmé, 'it doesn't vary: it's all tough. Needs to be kept at least a week. Unless you're doing a tagine or something and cooking it for days on end.' He made some reference to catering in a way that suggested he'd run a restaurant (a natural stage in a stage career). But before I could pursue it, the Waughs – the other guests – arrived.

During this pre-lunch conversation Nina mentioned a forthcoming party being given by the Hubert-Smythes. I had missed a chance at Bidfine's to find out more about them and their political views so was not going to let another opportunity pass. Mrs Waugh, when I raised the question, said she didn't know exactly but as a Democrat she always found herself opposed to Mr Hubert-Smythe. Alec said they were both Republicans. But even if they're extreme Republicans I don't (even now, having, since getting back, given it much thought) see how their views strike such horror in people there, who can hardly be called left-wing. I appealed to Esmé. He hinted it was all something to do with the idea that America was doomed and the Russians were going to take over the world. I said that was the view of many Americans: what was so strange? But I got nowhere at all.

Still, the name of the Hubert-Smythes inspired emotions in everyone and suddenly Esmé was conducting a spirited defence of the couple – against what I was no better able to make out.

'He's a magnificent man despite his politics. And she is an even more magnificent woman.'

'To have put up with him all these years,' someone – Nina? Forgotten – added.

Esmé ignored the interruption and went on with his defence. 'Jane Stray always maligns them, I know. But then she's a bitch.'

Alec Waugh jerked so erect at this he spilled his drink. 'Come now, sir,' he said. A whiff of the 18th century seemed to hover in the air.

His wife tried to soothe matters. 'Well, their daughter's absolutely delightful – that I can say. I taught her for a time and she wrote me saying she was going to be a teacher herself: "to pass on the good you taught me," she said.'

Mrs Waugh beamed and everyone seemed happy to let it rest

at that. I remained completely bewildered. And still am. I'd no chance to see the Hubert-Smythes, who were in Paris all the time we were there. Will I ever discover their secret?

The conversation turned to the house and what was going to happen to it. Nina said: 'Because it is *ad*jacent to the Royal Pal*ace* there will be pressure *to* find a purchaser suitable to *the* King.' (I.e. not European.)

I said at any rate Nettlewood was unlikely to be sold. A pause, then:

'Tommy Bidfine is a lovely man,' said Mrs Waugh. 'Such an aesthete. And a personality.'

'Fine chap,' said Alec. 'Came to see Mrs Févier every day in her last illness.'

Nina and Esmé were silent. Mrs Waugh said:

'So many people can't bear Tommy. I just don't understand it. I adore him.'

'And he adores that nephew of his,' said Alec. 'Brought him up like his own son. Poor chap lost both parents,' he observed to G and me. 'Tommy's always made a point of living somewhere accessible to him – when he was at school and so on. Even now he's here largely because the boy's stationed at Gib.'

This explained the importance of what Bidfine had called 'proximity to England'.

'Tommy's home is very bare,' Mrs Waugh reflected, 'and yet somehow it suits him exactly, don't you think? And that garden! Everyone says it used to be *such* a beautiful garden, but I think it's just wonderful the way he's let it run to seed…'

Another pause. Nina had sounded the terrace buzzer twice but no one had come to refill the drinks. She suggested we go in to lunch. (The thermometer I noticed read 73°F – warm enough to eat outside. But our hosts wore sweaters and the Waughs were in overcoats.)

Nina told Esmé to sit at the head of the table, but he said he preferred not to occupy Mrs Févier's chair. Nina sat there instead. It seemed odd being entertained in the house by a host and hostess neither of whom had any claim on it.

'At least meals will be more relaxed now,' said Nina. 'Edie used to bolt *her* food and we were expected to do *the* same. In church once when they brought her the communion wine she said "Finished that course. Next please." *It's* true.'

Esmé nodded. 'She once ate a three-course meal in forty-six seconds. We timed it.'

'Actually,' said Nina, 'she choked over brea*kfast* at the end. We slapped her back and so on but really it was *no* use.'

'Was there an inquest?' G ingenuously asked.

When we were all seated Esmé described the menu so that we could decide which wine to have with each course. 'It's coq au vin blanc,' he said, putting the accent on the 'blanc' to guide us, 'but before that we've artichokes with scrambled eggs and you're not supposed to drink wine at all with artichokes. Kills the taste, they say. Still, you could have some wine with the scrambled eggs bit, I suppose.'

Though he spoke lightly and ironically I got the impression that Esmé is a man who has known and knows about good living. On the terrace he drank gin without tonic. 'Beefeater's is too good to dilute with tonic, even if I liked tonic,' he said when I jokingly reproved him for such naked alcoholism. 'Really I prefer vodka. That's why I have gin strong – more like vodka that way.'

This bon vivant side of him extends to places. As we entered the dining room, someone pointed to the painting on the wall showing a man sitting under a plane tree in a little square dappled with sunshine. 'Provence, isn't it?' 'Yes, Arles, I should think,' said Esmé. 'The little Roman square there – though Nina knows Provence better than I do,' he added, still speaking ironically I thought.

'Your coq au vin is delicious, Esmé!' said Mrs Waugh with enthusiasm.

Esmé smiled thinly. 'Thyme and bay are the herbs,' he said.

'Really? I had a suspicion there was tarragon.'

'No. I dislike tarragon.'

'What is "tarragon"?' Nina asked. 'Oh, I know, it is *estragon*. Well, but it is *very* nice. But you have to know *how* much to put in.'

'I dislike it however much you put in,' said Esmé.

'Our tastes *in* herbs are very much *opposed*,' said Nina.

(I wonder if theirs was more successful than the partnership of Esmé with Miss Stray.)

The servants – a mournful pair of Moroccan women in traditional costume – weren't anything like as well-trained as Mrs Spicer's. She'd have been fairly smashing that gong of hers at their tardiness (Nina often had to ring two or three times before they appeared). And the sight of them serving men before women or hosts before guests would have driven her to distraction. You got to noticing things like that after a few weeks in Tangier.

But during the meal I was most astonished at how much lighter the atmosphere of the house felt than previously. It was as if all the dust and grime of a long and difficult life had been removed, letting the original bright colours of the place shine through again. Death had brought lightness to the living, whatever it had done for the dead woman herself. But among the living at the table the thought of death seemed quite attractive, as much, I suspected, on their own account as from any benefit derived from Mrs Févier's. This at any rate was the impression I formed from the lunch conversation, which was mainly about suicide.

There was nothing gloomy in this: quite the reverse. The table seemed about to take off from the zest with which all pressed G for details of the drugs required. G said valium and all those were no use; it had to be barbiturates – Seconal, for instance – which taken with alcohol would guarantee a fatal result.

'That's how Brian did it,' Esmé observed. 'Though he'd slashed his wrists to make sure – very Roman.'

'But he *didn't* die till five days later,' Nina objected.

'Didn't take enough,' said Esmé expertly. 'Or draw much blood, oddly enough. I helped pull him out of the bath.'

'I can't understand it,' said Mrs Waugh. 'He'd had a wonderful life. And he had a new book coming out in the fall.'

I wanted to ask who we were talking about, but Esmé's next remark stopped me in my tracks.

'Seconal and alcohol. That's how I shall do it,' he said.

That future tense had a paralysing effect, however much one subscribed to the idea that those who say they will never do.

Nina alone appeared unaffected. 'Well, there is no prob*lem* getting the Seconal here,' she said lightly, as if referring to the availability of cooking ingredients. 'In Morocco you *can* get

Seconal without *a* prescription,' she explained to G and me.

I couldn't resist saying it might be more difficult getting the alcohol, the way things were going. This effectively changed the subject, reminding everyone of the main alternative to suicide.

'If alcohol disappeared,' said Mrs Waugh, 'so would Alec – from Morocco.' Actually, she didn't put it quite like that: she said it would be a reason to make him leave the country.

After lunch we returned to the terrace for coffee (lukewarm – those servants again). Then Nina suggested everyone go and help themselves to any English books from the library. 'No *one* else will want them.'

I was going to follow the others but Esmé beckoned me to stay, asking me if I'd like a drink. I got the impression he didn't care to be alone even for a short time (he came along when Nina drove us back – 'for the ride' – though the evening turned chilly and it was quite an effort for him to get in and out of the car).

'All exiles are vicious,' he said when we were left alone together. 'But closet queens are more so. People like D H Lawrence and Willie Maugham, I mean. Only thing is to come out and have done with it.'

I said it was still difficult for pederasts, since the law remained in force.

'Didn't stop Norman Douglas,' he said. His thin lips parted in a smile that broadened into a laugh and set his whole face in motion, shaking tears from the watery blue eyes. 'I knew Douglas. I was only twenty at the time.' He paused; smiled again. 'He took me to see Lawrence who was living in the flat above his at Orioli's – the Italian publisher. But Lawrence was too ill to see me by then.'

We talked mainly of plays and pederasty.

'I used to write plays,' Esmé said. 'With absolutely no success whatsoever,' he added, in the tone of someone vouchsafing his credentials. 'I wrote a play about Lady Hester Stanhope. Sent it to Edith Evans – who I used to know. She said it wasn't the kind of part she wanted to play.'

'I should have thought it ideal,' I said.

'So should I,' said Esmé.

He smoked his cigarette and we looked at the view of Tangier over which a golden glow was developing as the sun started sinking.

'I was at Oxford with John Gielgud,' he said after a pause; the glow perhaps evoking this period of his past. 'I knew lots of others who've become stars. When I lived in Jamaica, I knew Noël Coward.'

I thought of Spicer who had not known the future famous even when they were at Oxford. I thought also how haphazard the whole business of fame was. Kenneth Tynan had once described Gielgud as 'a great actor from the neck upwards'. Gielgud's reputation rested very largely on his voice. Yet Esmé's was very similar. So for that matter was the broadcaster Brian Johnston's. All three had set out as matinée idols (for Esmé, despite present appearances, had clearly been that). But one had made the leap to international acclaim, while even Johnston had managed celebrity in some form. Only Esmé was nothing at all. Hadn't reached a position that, in a word of his generation, could be called 'middling' even. Still I found his failure much more interesting than Gielgud's or Johnston's success.

'I read the reviews,' Esmé went on. 'I always know what's going on. There was a play the other day that interested me, at the Theatre Upstairs.' (The mere sound of this from his lips seemed wildly anachronistic, as if Henry Irving were described as a television personality. I wondered as well if Esmé had the remotest idea of the standing of the Theatre Upstairs.) 'I used to do a bit with the Tangier Dramatic Society,' he added. 'Now defunct.'

'Like so much in *Tang*er,' said Nina, who'd come back on to the terrace.

'Including me,' said Esmé. 'We're all too old for the parts and anyway we have to wear glasses just to read the script – couldn't possibly remember it of course. Though Anthony Crashaw does one or two things still.'

'He is the Queen of Tangier Society,' Nina informed me, going.

'Literally,' said Esmé. 'He says: "They all come here social-climbing and when they reach the top of the tree, what do they find? Screaming old me!"' Esmé laughed again, but this time the trickling tears merged with a stream of saliva which he was unable to control. Dabbing this up, he said: 'Actually I've just had an idea but I don't know whether to write it as a play or a story. What d'you think is better?'

Before I could answer (or make some pretence at answering so unanswerable a question) he asked me if I would take back to London two plays of his and get someone to put them on.

'They're rather experimental. I sent them to the Royal Shakespeare but they sent them back. I also showed them – oh, ten years back – to that bastard who ran the Nottingham Playhouse. I knew him once. Who do I mean? Forget. He never even replied. I had to write to get them back. I should be interested to hear what you think of them. Send them wherever you think is suitable. And if you have no luck, just throw them away. I've no use for them here.'

Before we left he gave me the two plays. They are called 'Black Sea Sailing' and 'Lament for the Leopard's Siblings'. Both 'By ESME ST CLAIR'.

The others had returned to watch the sunset and Esmé mixed cocktails, not trusting the servants to do it. Everyone seemed distinctly melancholy, the thought clearly in all minds that there would be only a few more occasions like this before the house was sold. 'May well be the last lunch I cook here,' said Esmé. 'Don't know what'll happen to me now. Nowhere to go, no money to buy anything of my own. 'Spect I'll fall to pieces.' His mouth fell open in a forlorn smile, his tongue as usual flabbily hovering between his lips. His thin frame shook a little, less from laughter, I thought, this time. He covered his emotion by helping himself to a drink, 'as we're all having another round, I see'. The remark reminded me of Miss Stray's at the Brigadier's lunch soon after we arrived: '…if we're all going to get blotto,' she'd said in a sardonic tone that, like Esmé's, hid her underlying sadness. I saw now how similar they were; and why living together had not been a success.

Mrs Waugh lifted her head to heaven and, closing her eyes, said: 'Why do things have to change? I like things always to stay the same.'

At that moment a locust appeared in the garden before us. We all looked at it, reduced to silence by so obvious a symbol.

'They're terribly *de*structive,' said Nina at last.

She got up to catch the locust. 'You have to take off its head,' she said as she drew near to it. But it flew away, disturbed by her approach.

Esmé smiled. 'It's had a lucky escape,' he said.

'Let's hope we do *the* same,' said Nina.

We all drank to that.

Part Three

Tangier: Grand Hotel Villa de France

24 April 198–

The door-boy and waiters all recognised us. Like the big scene from *Hello, Dolly*. Greg almost in tears.

We have a different room but still with 'The View'. The hotel – now Moroccan-owned – seems unchanged: uitsmeyer hollandais on the menu, hangover from the ancien régime; and as before white wine brought for red. (This I anticipated by deliberately ordering the opposite. They then brought the wrong mineral water: 'Gas?' 'Oui, gas.' 'Bien. Sans gas.')

Place very empty even at this later season. But: an extension is being built... (*Mediterranean Winter Resorts*: 'the management has always shown itself alive to modern requirements. It has recently laid down a tennis court.')

Longing to know what's happened to everyone. Correspondence these last five years has been erratic to say the least.

26 April

The mood on the streets is much as before. A man passes: 'You want to fuck later?' A boy calls: 'Sixty-nine is good number – like to try?' 'Big tits?' whispers another. (This one followed us along the Boulevard making gestures with his fingers and interspersing the sound 'fook' with a price-scale. It began at thirty dirhams and ended with 'Cigarette?' I thought of GIs in post-war Italy.)

In most respects, though, have noticed a distinct tightening-up – presumably the need for tourists means they're sensitive to tourist needs. (Cf. Franco's Spain.) Certainly nothing like the pestering of old. I can go out without my *Matin du Sahara*. I still buy it though. As I have throughout this trip. I like to see what 'S.M.' is up to. (Besides, the English papers couldn't be more boring: full of endless 'spying revelations'.)

Today the *Matin* announces that S.M. is setting up an Académie Marocaine – to be modelled on the French one. Another nail in the coffin of literature.

The food at the hotel is no better for the Moroccans. It is no worse either. (But after the past weeks of the Grands Hotels du Sud, we know the truth about all hotel cooking in Morocco.) So it's back to the old routine: Porte's, Claridge, Parade, or any combination of the three. Today lunch in the Parade garden. All set up for the summer. Several old regulars drowning their sorrows. (Among them Brandon/Brendon – who has already rung up about bridge.) Madame was not in evidence. Dead? No one seemed to know. A parrot in a cage said 'Watch it' continually. A Pest appeared waving horribly unenticing wares. But feebly. None of the old bravura. 'Je mange!' said G. 'Tu manges?' Pest repeats. 'Pour que je mange, moi, faut qu' t'achètes un cadeau.'

We gave him some dirhams.

(No reply from the Févier villa. Where are Nina and Esmé?)

27 April

To Asilah – *for lunch.* (No news yet of the Waughs.) On the way, reminisced about our trip there last time with Rev. Jones and Miss Mare (no news of them either).

The place much bigger, more prosperous, less pretty. Returned to same restaurant. Same sole, brought to the table. No wine. ('Now Moroccan-owned.') Luckily we'd come prepared with a bottle bought in Tangier. (Had similar experiences in the south.)

Beside us, young earnest-looking Swedes haggled in English with a derelict Moroccan for some worthless-looking goods. Talked about 'the profit margin' and 'a good price for *us*'. Drank Coke, counted out notes, spoke loud to get above the waves. A passing black boy slapped one of them on the buttocks, saying 'Salut!' Black boy laughed. Swedes frowned.

Afterwards sat over mint tea. A few Pests around but I'd left *Matin* in a prominent position. One approached, said please, he did not want to pester (seeing reflex of my hand towards *Matin*). Pests in Morocco gave Moroccans bad name. He was not such a one. I invited him to sit. He did. Then asked me to write a letter to his wife.

I instantly picked up *Matin*. Waved it in his face. He said, please, *not* pester, wife was *English*. Worked at a restaurant in

Camberley. Did I know Camberley? I said not at all. But I said I was sorry they had to live so far apart. He agreed it was sad. But perhaps, I suggested, their lack of a common language mitigated the loss of one another's company. He began to look sheepish. Would he be so kind, I enquired, as to show me the last letter from his 'wife', that I might pen a suitable reply?

He admitted his wife lived in Asilah. The letter was to a nurse in Leytonstone. (Did I know Leytonstone?) They had met at a restaurant in Camberley.

I said I would write his letter. But letter-writing in Morocco cost money. How many dirhams would he pay me? He looked very offended. Said this was for *friendship*. Shook my hand.

Decided to amuse myself. Scrawled string of Freudian symbols, innuendoes, double entendres. Guaranteed to arouse a freezer. He hovered alongside. Drooled on about 'making it good'.

I assured him I was making it good.

'She will like?'

'She won't have seen the like.'

'She will come?'

'In a flash.'

He went off studying my handiwork, looking bemused. Not half as bemused as the nurse will in Leytonstone.

Later another one appeared. Encouraged by success of first. Asked me to write to a man in Bayswater. He was minding his house in Asilah.

My blood was up, my fingers twitched, my mind raced... *Car stolen... house burnt to ground... all property lost...*

But G – spoilsport – restrained me.

At the station they said the Casablanca Pullman was an hour late. So we sat in the sunshine watching the Atlantic. (You adjust to things here. And besides, coming back by the Casablanca Pullman was the reason we'd gone to Asilah by train.)

Opposite, seated by a road-sign ('No left turn') a Biblical figure wrote a letter for a man who paid in twigs (so much for my hope of dirhams).

Suddenly a jeep screeches to a halt. Top Brass descend, prance up to station, enter, collar station-master, who is on phone – 'Allo? Allo?' – for news of Casablanca Pullman. (Turns out to be *two* hours late. We came back by taxi. There are limits.)

Minutes pass. All reappear. Stand conferring. Finally return to jeep. Exeunt Top Brass, top speed.

More minutes pass. (We are still sitting in the sunshine watching the Atlantic. Biblical figure still writing letter.) Sudden flash. Convoy of cars. Sirens blare. Lights blaze. Our view for a camera-shutter fraction of a second cut off.

Then silence...

And again we are sitting in the sunshine, watching the Atlantic...

Biblical figure carries on writing... Client carries on dictating...

'You have seen the Sultan?' the station-master asks.

(He is about the only person we *have* seen. But: off now to Miss Stray's... Invites us round 'for the lowdown'.)

28 April

She looked exactly the same. If anything, improved. Repeated herself hardly at all. Now she's seventy-five she's upped her official age to ninety. 'No one believes it. Cheers me no end.' The drain flowed freely. (I think the plumbing at least has been overhauled.)

'Only got beer,' she said gloomily. The flat was very bare, her belongings all packed up. 'You've just caught me. I'm off to Spain next week. They've finally found me a hovel to end m'days in.' Short gurgle, then: 'So where've you been? Go over the Atlas, did you?'

'Three times.'

'Tizi-n-Test?'

'Yes.'

'Tizi-n-Tichka?'

'Yes.'

'Bet you didn't do Tizi-n-Tarhemt?'

'Pass-of-the-She-Camel? Yes.'

Miss Stray sipped her beer. 'I did all that once,' she said pensively. 'Anyway, let's have a gossip. That's what you've come for! I know!'

The lowdown:

First shock – the Waughs have gone. Less on Alec's account than Virginia's: her health had deteriorated. Then some trouble with the lease of their flat. 'Usual levering out of Europeans,' Miss Stray said. So they've gone back to Florida. Sad. Shall miss not seeing them.

Second shock – the British Consulate (where we had that final glimpse of Alec last time) – is closed. The Thatcher cuts spread far and wide. Miss Stray said everyone is very upset. ('It was the Conservatives! That's what they can't get over!') She said it was the one British centre left here. 'We're not like the French and Spanish with their own clubs and things. *They*'ll be in their element now. Well, there's just not enough of us to make it worthwhile. Someone said they should make it a British-in-Tangier museum – like the Americans with their old legation. Or else turn it into flats for derelicts like me. Don't expect they will. Probably knock it down.'

First non-shock – Miss Mare and Rev. Jones are married. 'It was the highlight of the winter. The Bish came out specially. They say we've all got to go very Câtholic and start praying to Our Lady of Tangier!'

Second non-shock – The Féviers made Nina leave the villa. She is now in a flat over the Fez market here. (This has some significance apparently, but Miss Stray didn't elaborate.) Nina is giving a party, to which we are invited. It's being held at Harvey Lambert's house – which means we'll see *him* again: whatever the logistics of his diary.

Nothing on Bidfine – on whom, though, Miss S. is not keen. Must ring him.

'I'll see you at the party – if not before,' Miss Stray said as we left. (As usual everyone is seeing everyone else.) But if Miss Stray is going to the party, presumably Esmé St Clair won't be. No reason to suppose their estrangement has ended. Miss Stray didn't mention him. And we didn't dare to. But as Nina had to leave the Févier villa, he can't have hung on there. Is he still here? (Is he still *alive…*?)

A bizarre incident at the Parade (where we went for dinner – it was the Halibut Solferino here tonight). At the table next to ours an elderly Englishman sat gloomily eating. It was the one we saw often there on the first trip. Always gloomily eating. (Mostly gloomily drinking.)

An extremely good-looking young Moroccan sat down at his table. He cheered up considerably. A pleasant diner à deux seemed in prospect. But suddenly a quarrel had developed. At first it was friendly, almost playful. Then all at once the elderly Englishman was on his feet, his face gaunt and tense. 'Why are you drinking beer?' he asks the Moroccan. 'Because I like it,' the boy replies. Englishman sniffs like harassed schoolmaster. 'You may look Midi French, but you're a Moor,' he says in an old-fashioned fatal tone. 'And Moors aren't allowed to touch alcohol. They're not my laws,' he went on, 'and they're not Lillie's laws,' he added, with a glance at the raddled fixture at the bar (which I was glad to see in existence still) In its usual state of alcoholic ennui the fixture seemed unaware of the point he was making. 'They're Moroccan laws though,' he continued, 'and it's incumbent on you to uphold them. What's going to happen not just to you but to Lillie and me if a policeman comes in and catches you drinking?'

The boy said quietly that he wasn't a Moslem. The Englishman dismissed this with a contemptuous snort (or it may have been a gastric protest), gathered his glass and bottle (abandoning less vital equipment) and stomped off with the bewildering exit line, 'I'm going to find myself a place instead of this table which was *my* table till you joined it.'

The whole episode had the air of a scene from the kind of B-movie which might have had a Parade Bar setting. For a moment the thought crossed my mind that this might be a cabaret act, an atmosphere number put on by the management to re-create the Tangier of legend (sort of thing you see in the London clubs: Upper-Class Queen has Row with Moroccan Boyfriend in Public – Huge Scandal! Etc.) So that's what it was like in the good old days: feasting with panthers... purple sins...

Ho-hum...

(Tried ringing Bidfine. No answer.)

29 April

News of Esmé. Came by chance.

We had asked for lunch by the pool (which I now realise is the tennis court of yore: more plus ça change...) The head waiter – the same Grand Vizier figure from before – said we could not be served outside. I said we'd often eaten outside last time. He said that was under the old management; but conceded we could have '*un* plat' by the pool. I said that was all we wanted (the food here hardly encourages indulgence). But the other waiters came out and laid our table for a full meal. The head waiter watched. When they'd finished he added salt and pepper pots. We were then served a three-course lunch.

As we ate, a couple appeared who, apart from a tall grey-haired man who reads Dick Francis, are the only other people here. They look models of what the hotel brochure calls 'individual travellers' who give the place its 'distinguished atmosphere'. He: panama hat, sketchbook, hoarse Cecil Parker voice, retired civil servant looks. She: sunhat (floppy), pleated skirt; writes diary in very neat script. I had placed them as silver wedding rather than honeymoon (brochure: '*idéal pour voyages de noce*').

But I was wrong. 'We were recently married,' the woman informed us. 'They said this hotel was ideal for honeymoons. We've been here a month.' I said we spent a month here once. 'When it was still run by the Dutch couple? They say it's not so good now it's owned by Moroccans.' I said they would. (*Mediterranean Winter Resorts*: 'of late years the Villa de France has gone through vicissitudes, but still holds its own as the favourite sojourn of invalids, artists and literary people'.) 'Well, *we*'ve loved every minute,' the woman went on. 'Have you been to church? It's such a pretty church. And you meet all the British residents. They're *charming* people. We play bridge with them. Actually, the main bridge bod's an American.' I asked if he was called Brandon Brendon. She said she thought it was Brendon Brandon. Anyway, he was a *delightful* person. So were they all, all delightful people. 'I rather dropped a brick on Sunday though, I mistook someone for eighty who turned out to be ten years younger! He was most indignant. He's an ex-actor. He appeared with Noël Coward...'

Esmé has just phoned.

We were having dinner (we ate here tonight: the waiters look at you so appealingly. Not their fault; they deserve better). As before the dining room had a melancholy atmosphere, like the villa of a monarch in exile. But – there was musak playing... Anyhow, Esmé said he was 'kicked out of the Févier villa in the most unpleasant way'. He is now living at the Pension Buonavita. He was most anxious to know what had happened to those plays of his I took back. I said I was eating, could I ring him back? He said, did I know he was writing a pantomime?

He is giving a party (to which we are invited). He is not sure if he is going to Nina's party. He didn't know 'who else' was going: i.e. if Miss Stray is.

Had coffee (always bad here) on the terrace of the Claridge. The Midi-French-looking Moroccan boy from the Parade incident was there. He sat with another, more Moroccan, Moroccan. They spoke Arabic, then French. Then the Midi-French Moroccan, glancing in our direction, said: 'Let's speak English. I prefer speaking English.' They spoke English. Then the Midi-French-looking boy leant across, smiled, asked for a cigarette. I said I was sorry, I didn't smoke cigarettes. Coffee was very good.

(I was sitting in the courtyard here finishing my cigar – breeze gently swaying the palms, staff going off duty bidding good-night – when the atmosphere was violently disturbed by the raucous sound of French en masse. Into the courtyard came porters bearing mounds of luggage, followed by a large group of people wearing badges and looking not at all like 'individual travellers'; creating the very opposite of a 'distinguished atmosphere'.

Is this the beginning of the end...?)

30 April

We saw the honeymoon couple in the medina. He wore a solar topé and white tropical suit and held a stick. She said she must have a hat. He said: 'We can't go chasing about after a hat, dear.' When we got back to the hotel they were struggling with the wrought-iron gates. A Moroccan in djellaba and fez was assisting them. He kept saying 'Open, Sesame!' I get the impression the honeymoon is over.

The tall grey-haired man who reads Dick Francis spoke to us this evening.

We were sitting on the terrace over port and cigars and he approached saying it was 'nice to see a good old British tradition being kept up'. We said, was his Dick Francis interesting? He then said we'd got good tans. ('Need to work on your backs though.') Invited us to his room for a drink.

He is Dutch-Australian; which sounds South African. A surfing, outbacking sort of man. Works for a company in Casa.

His room is small and confined and without a view (company economy). His family lives in Casa (company policy). They occasionally visit (company compassion). The hotel provides a bigger room.

The place was strewn with bottles and clothes, suitcases and carpets. Suggested a life of frantic activity followed by bouts of ennui. Turned out he's a salesman. He said Morocco is a wonderful country for salesmen. The people really love haggling. They make a day of it. He's been everywhere here. Has a purchase for every place. He showed us them. Each one has a label saying where it was bought, how much was paid, difference from the asking price and how long the deal took. At this level, he said, buying and selling was an art. (I said, no thanks, I wouldn't have a refill.)

Actually he told us a lot about conditions here now. Gross lack of health facilities. Half the children dying. People saving to buy a sheep. (Labour disputes over sheep for annual feast.) He said you see only a fraction of it because of the strong family ties: girls in his company's factory at Casa provided often for a dozen or more. The company laid on some medical care but, yes, largely here for cheap labour. He said things had gone steadily downhill ever since the French left. Now the Sultan is raising taxes for the Polisario war. He said there were no more than eighty thousand nomads in the disputed areas – 'who don't care who gets the territory. But the Algerians and Moroccans do: there may be phosphates. Very nice for Morocco and useful for Algeria if they could set up a puppet state there which gave them an outlet to the Atlantic and a chance to explore the phosphates through it.'

He thought the Moroccans were doing badly in the war.

Recently Goulimime was shelled. The Polisario were expelled afterwards and a great Moroccan victory announced (I could imagine the headlines in the *Matin*). 'But it was a real humiliation having the enemy penetrate hundred and fifty miles into the country.' Still, he was sure there'd be an 'accommodation' – with both sides saving face. S.M. and the Algerian president had met 'by chance' at Mecca last year. 'They'll have worked something out. Anyhow, whatever happens, Mauritania – being the poor relation – is bound to be the one to lose out.'

'The game's up in Morocco,' he said at one point. 'You know, Europeans on the way out, Arabs on the way in. *But* – a new game is on. Sure, there's the cosmetic changes – street-signs and what have you. Gives everything a respectable Islamic façade. Hassan even wants to make Wednesday a fully observed holy day like Friday – just to add to our problems. But that's not religion. That's politics. He's out to guarantee his throne. He knows consumerism has taken firm root here. They don't object to material goods. Just to Hassan's distribution of them. After all, it's not so very different from the old mercantile Arab culture. I prefer the Berbers in the south. You've been in the south? Yeah, they're nice people. But they're worried as hell here,' he went on. 'They need the tourists and the tourists aren't coming. Not the Americans anyhow. Iranian crisis finished 'em off. Young Moroccan I know had his American girlfriend break off their engagement over it. Mind you, her parents were always against it. The engagement, I mean. Yes, they're worried all right here.'

I pressed him a little on the politics, hoping we might touch on the Hubert-Smythes and their views (we've heard nothing about them so far). But like most here, he wouldn't be drawn. 'What you say can easily get back to the Government. One day you wake up and find yourself expelled – or worse: put in jail.' He paused; said: 'Or else one day you don't wake up at all. So many damn factions here you never know which one you're on the wrong side of. Sure, they're mostly anti-Sultan. Specially the young ones. They want a republic and a fairer share of the goodies. But they're not all the same way anti-Sultan. There's pro-Western anti-Sultan, anti-Western anti-Sultan, anti-Islam anti-Sultan, anti-Western anti-Islam anti-Sultan (they're probably

the best hope for democracy – which never *had* a hope in Iran).
Yeah, you name it, they're against it. And even if *you*'re against
what they're against, they'll most likely think you're a government
spy.'

He made it sound a precarious sort of life.

'Needless to say, the country's full of corruption. And nepotism.
And sheer stupidity. The Minister of Agriculture's lived all his life
in a town. Hasn't one hell of an idea about farming. But he's a
cousin of Hassan.' He said he spent half his time bribing people.
'Ten dirhams – what's that? A British pound? – still a lot of money
in this country. Five hours' work. Very welcome if you're a
customs official. Mind you –' (He smiled; well, contorted his
mouth.) '– I've bribed plenty of customs officials in England!'

(Still no reply from Bidfine's…)

1 May

Nina's party. It's turned out an eventful evening. When it rains
here, it pours (it is tonight); and when things happen, they
cascade. Usual problem (cf. last time): how to get it down? Start
at the beginning. Or try to.

Nina – as before, bright and hectic but looking ill and aged, I
thought – drove us to Harvey Lambert's house for tea before the
party got going. The route took us along Rue Shakespeare. I said I
was surprised it hadn't been renamed.

'It won't be,' said Nina. 'The editor of *Matin du Sahara* lives
here and doesn't want to change his letter-heading.'

A little further on she pointed to a romantic house on the
Atlantic side. 'That's where *I* used to live,' she said. 'It's a very
beautiful house. I miss it,' she added, and there was a pause. I had
not pressed Nina for details about her past last time, realising
sensitive ground must lie between the death of her husband and
her return to Tangier in a new capacity. (On our first visit
Tommy Bidfine provided some information, prompted by my
simple question about her surname, Dupresne. 'Dorset people.
One of those posh English-French names with the treacherous
pronunciations – you say "Doopreen". Which rather sums up the
family.')

But now Nina herself had touched on her own history, I thought I might pursue it a little. I asked how long she'd been away before coming back to Tangier.

'Oh, *some* years,' she said vaguely. 'It was a kind of in*ter*im period for me.' (Bidfine: 'Worked in some sort of shop, I believe.') Nina jerked the steering wheel round as if to indicate the change of direction in her life. 'Then I had the offer from Mrs Févier *to* be her companion. Seemed *the* natural thing to do. Besides, Europe was *im*possible for me. It was *too* cold and too *ex*pensive.' (Bidfine: 'Very little money. Unlike me!')

'But *of* course it was a ghastly *mis*take,' Nina casually concluded as we turned in at the gates of Lambert's house. 'It is one thing to live in *a* lovely place like this,' she said, applying heavy break; 'quite another *to* live in a flat above *the* Fez market.' We came to an abrupt halt. 'Also, I have been *quite* ill since you *were* here. When they *in*sisted I leave the villa I shared *a* flat with a very *dear* friend, who drove me com*plete*ly mad!' I made a mental note not to ask any more questions. As it turned out, I didn't have to.

We stood before an enormous house, Moroccan in style but utterly Victorian in extravagance. Harvey Lambert appeared on the steps of the entrance, looking wildly out of place in the grandiose surroundings, so strong an impression did I retain of him from Fez as occupant of Room One at the Hotel Majestic.

'You're here! You're here!' he called joyously. For some reason I thought of the Valkyries. Once we were inside he seemed entirely in his element. The atmosphere of the house was very cool and dank with a smell of wet clay like a museum on some ancient site. He led us curator-like through the echoing rooms, saying, 'The place is in a frightful state – I camp out in the south-facing room.'

To reach this outpost of civilisation we had to negotiate huge areas of cluttered disorder, every item of which exuded not former magnificence – everything from furniture and books to dinner services and coats of armour was magnificent still – but a once orderly world now in hopeless disarray.

The place was not a museum (far too chaotic for that) but not an inch of it did anything less than reek hugely of the past. It was like walking through the backstage store of an opera house, wandering among sets and props for innumerable old productions. Everything is there, every last detail and implement needed to put the scene back on the stage. Only the actors are missing, to set it in motion. You could imagine Lambert's parents (they lived there before him) in the dining room with their servants and guests, the whole household in full function, according to the workings of a secure, vital and seemingly unending society; all these stacked-away chairs, tables and piled-up plates in their proper places, like the people occupying and serving around them. Now the whole jigsaw had been dismantled in a way that made it impossible to reassemble. All the pieces were intact but the circumstances on which it depended for its ordered construction were gone for ever.

Lambert, less owner than keeper of all these exhibits, did not so much walk as ramble through the house. Stooping, in grey flannels and a shapeless tweed jacket, the cotton wool over the lost eye almost a badge of office, he looked the ideal figure to preside over the excavated remains of this vanished world.

We reached the inhabited zone and entering it I noticed the odour of wet clay, which pervaded the rest of the building, gave way here to the pleasant perfume of cedar-wood burning in a Swedish tiled stove. The room, which opened on to the garden, was long and no less dishevelled than the others: but with all the signs of everyday life – newspapers, ashtrays and cushions; books on early civilisations. We sat down in low, graceful armchairs and Lambert, still smiling with delight that we were there (though he kept his diary handy) moved a pile of *New Yorkers* from the table and served tea on it. We talked generally for a bit about the intervening years (on neither side specially eventful) but the conversation soon slipped into esoteric channels. This was largely my fault.

I had idly re-set my pedometer and seeing it Lambert asked me if I had a *bio*meter. 'It measures the physical, mental and *psychic* states of a person,' he said excitedly. 'In Japan they swear by them. If all three measurements come below a certain level they forbid pilots to fly.'

Thus launched, he came up with one or two mythological tit-bits but, perhaps remembering our evening at Fez, switched suddenly to funny stories about professors of classics. There was something touching in the way even Lambert's store of humour was centred in antiquity.

It took Nina's organised mind to steer us to more pressing topics. 'It's very good *of* you, Harvey, to hold *my* party here,' she said pointedly after a tale of washing going astray in the department of Egyptology.

'Not at all! Not at all!' Lambert said quickly, as usual giving his attention wholeheartedly to the new matter in hand. 'The drink's been delivered,' he went on, 'though they say the black market's drying up. The customs at Ceuta have tightened up.'

'Oh? Was extra cost *in*curred?'

Lambert looked sheepishly at the floor. 'Well, I had to fork up another hundred and fifty, but really—'

Nina opened her handbag and counted out the notes. Lambert took them from her outstretched hand. 'Thanks very much,' he said in the grateful tone I remembered from our visit to Nettlewood last time.

Straightaway Nina said: 'Harvey, why *don't* you take these boys for a walk in the garden. Mrs Spicer is lending me *her* servants who will arrive here any minute so we *can* make all the preparations.'

Lambert looked relieved, less I thought at Nina's tactful change of subject (which might have been subtler had she not actually counted out the notes) than at being assigned a task that would give pleasure to his guests instead of one (preparations for the party) at which he didn't excel. He smiled and his eye lit up so much that for a moment one forgot the significance of the cotton wool.

His new enthusiasm was not hard to explain. As so often the garden turned out to be the highlight of even this house. Lambert led us out of the room over moss-covered steps that began at the windows and descended through a series of arbours down the hill to the sea. The garden rambles off in every direction – flowers running in wild profusion everywhere – and between the cascading trees sudden breathtaking glimpses of the Atlantic and the jagged line of the coast with its inlay of coves and bays. Wherever you go you hear the sound of the waves. (Even Bidfine doesn't have the sound of the waves.)

As we walked, Lambert interspersed descriptions of all the flowers and shrubs with the usual recondite references. At one moment he was pointing out the resemblance of a certain species to a banana tree, at the next reflecting on Hittite weaponry. All the time we were looking down at the waves crashing against the rocks. Lambert made no concession to the scene, though far from indifferent to it. He seemed to find it a stimulus to rarefied discussion. As we strolled along the top of the cliffs he explained the difference between the Naib and the Mendoub. He described how the house was intended for the former of these officials. His parents had bought it and completed it after the Franco-Spanish takeover. He showed us a picture of them in Bombay in 1897.

'Have you met Monty Caucus?' he asked suddenly.

I shook my head. (Carefully: the wind was strong on the brink of the precipice.) G, who looked pale, took a few steps away. Lambert ambled along the edge, saying: 'Caucus is the name of a Moroccan Jewish family. They provisioned the British Fleet here. In reward the Prince Regent gave them the freedom of the British Empire. Monty Caucus is the latest in the line.'

We both nodded vigorously, feeling movement was safe again. We were heading back to the house. Cornwall with a climate, I thought; that's the real appeal of the place.

'Do you know the Great McLean?' Lambert enquired as we climbed back up the steps. I said he hadn't been on the Bishop's list. 'Oh, he's long dead,' said Lambert. 'He commanded the Sultan's forces at the turn of the century. There's a portrait of him in the Minzah Hotel. He lived in the house at the other end of this street,' he added, as though referring to a terrace in the suburbs. 'Nina lived in it. That was before she went off with the old English major.'

For a moment the casualness of this remark made me miss its significance. 'Old English Major' struck me in the same way as 'Monty Caucus' and 'the Great McLean': another colourful Tangier character. (The tune of 'The Galloping Major' even went through my head.) But Lambert's next remarks, equally casual, allowed no such mistake.

'She met him in the Fez market,' he said. 'They had a most romantic conversation. Went off to Scotland together. But apparently he thought she had money and she thought he did and really neither of them had any. And Nina has to have someone with money because under her husband's will she loses his if she gets married again. So it all ended. But now Nina has a flat overlooking the Fez market where it began. Isn't that extraordinary? Are you interested in coincidence?' he concluded. 'I have numerous books on the subject. I find it utterly fascinating.'

His face beamed with the enthusiasm he showed for all his esoteric interests. What for many would have been juicy gossip, Lambert saw in objective, unemotional terms, like a doctor viewing a patient (or, come to that, a writer looking at life in general).

In this respect Lambert is unusual – which is not saying much of a man who's unusual in every respect. Tangier has, in my experience, certainly lived up to its reputation for gossip. But then whatever voyeuristic, prurient interest the lives of the famous arouse, there's still nothing to beat news of your own immediate circle – who are famous to you. It seems to satisfy an almost confessional need for gossip people have. Which I find not unnatural. It's caginess – both public and private – that most worries me.

But I'm getting distracted. And can't afford to. There is much to relate. But in the morning. Tonight has been very exhausting...

2 May

So:

Back at the house Nina's driving organisation had transformed into a model of order the room we had left chaotic barely an hour before. Mrs Spicer's servants were already in possession and the world of Harvey Lambert had disappeared from view. Glasses, bowls of olives and biscuits, plates of sandwiches and cheese were now in evidence. Ancient civilisations had once again vanished from the surface of the earth. Everything now suggested the cocktail hour.

'Isn't it an absolutely beautiful garden?' Nina said as we came in.

'Well, yours was even nicer in my opinion,' Lambert said modestly. 'I was saying you used to live in Caid McLean's house.'

'Oh yes,' Nina said shortly. A pause, then: 'Well, but shall we have *a* drink?'

As she ordered drinks from Mrs Spicer's servants, Lambert said: 'Of course, this part of Tangier is very unlikely to change.' He said 'change' with the slight shudder everyone brings to that horror verb here. 'You see, the road is just a narrow lane and the steepness of the Atlantic side makes more building impossible. Also the government want to prevent the kind of coastal development that happened in Spain.'

'Yes, *per*haps,' Nina reflected. 'But people *have* said once *the* same of Franco. And *I* think it is terrible that the road past the *Queen* Mother's house outside Tangier is closed per*man*ently when she comes there a single time only in *the* year. And the King not at all since they tried *to* kill him here.'

People were beginning to arrive. ('Parties are early here now,' Nina explained. 'We are very *se*curity conscious.')

As we stood sipping our drinks I found myself almost trembling with anticipation at the thought of seeing again a group of people I knew hardly at all yet retained so strong an impression of. But to begin with I recognised no one and the room was filling up quickly, quite a few elegant Moroccans among the first arrivals. I became quite anxious, wondering if those I most wanted to see had for some reason stayed away. (This turned out the case with Tommy Bidfine. Nina told me she wanted him to come but 'he seldom *goes* out now. Up on that Mountain *of* his he is *the* last of the Plantagenets'. Must ring him again today.)

Suddenly my fears were allayed. My dramatic instinct came to the rescue, alerting me to the fact that these 'beginners' were the minor characters! Tangier society obeyed the rules of the old well-made plays. Here were those useful small-part actors brought on first – almost sacrificial in function – to provide all one needed to know about the major characters yet to appear. Talking with these people thus followed a strictly expositional pattern: 'So-and-so is coming who knows So-and-so-else.' 'X will be here who was married to Y but now lives with Z.' '*You* know – the one who – *that's* right. Well, apparently now he…'

In this exposition occupations were alone omitted; few here having them. (One man Nina introduced me to as 'a fellow writer'. He had been a journalist in Sweden. 'I was there for three years,' he said impressively. No word of the remaining sixty-odd.)

But the principal character referred to in these opening exchanges was none other than (Nina's phrase from last time) the Queen of Tangier Society: the Hon. Anthony Crashaw (still can't recall which duke or viscount or whatever he's related to). It was rumoured that he was putting in at least a guest appearance.

'You are very fortunate to get him,' someone said to Nina.

Nina demurred in the way only the French can. Nothing so crude as a shrug of the shoulder. A mere down-curling of a lip. 'Well, but I *sup*pose this house is grand *e*nough for him,' she said.

Meanwhile G and I had met a few people on holiday here (including the honeymoon couple from the hotel who'd somehow ended up there and seemed a bit overwhelmed by the surroundings). I had placed among these visitors a young Scottish couple, positively infant by Tangerine standards. I soon saw I was wrong. They must be new residents. They talked constantly of 'Tanjawis' and 'Tangieros'. They had a delightfully criminal air; a vitality quite at odds with respectable life. The man said he'd got away from the rat race. For ten years he'd been a car salesman in Glasgow. Now he was going to write. He understood I was a writer. I said I was. He said I had a peeling nose. His wife said she found it *ap*pealing. He asked G to go outside with him 'to talk about a medical matter'. They went off together. I was left with the girl. She said she had two children. If they were in Scotland they'd be hooligans by now. Whereas here they spoke fluent French and Arabic.

My attention began to wander. A bloated figure in a sombrero and long draping cloak with a pleat down the back had entered. That it was male became apparent when it took off the sombrero and revealed a serrated face and a mass of black hair discreetly concealing it. He swayed rather than walked round the room calling people darling and kissing almost everyone present.

'Do you *know* Brandon Brendon?' the Scottish girl asked me. I said he'd rung about bridge a dozen times or so.

'He's a great bridge player,' the Scottish girl said.

(The honeymoon couple must have been sensing more than a change of convention in their 'delightful' acquaintance.)

At that moment I glanced away and at once Brandon's antics were eclipsed for me by the sight of who was standing in the doorway.

It was unfortunate for Esmé that his entrance coincided with the Brandon Brendon performance which had become the focal point of the room. Esmé stood, leaning heavily on his stick, as much at attention as his shaky frame allowed, waiting to be observed. He even went out and came in again, hoping for more success second time round. But apart from me absolutely no one was looking in his direction. All eyes were concentrated on the kind of minuet Brendon was executing with one of the servants.

Perhaps Esmé's timing had never been the strong point of his stage career; but even without Brendon's distraction the lack of attention accorded him could have been explained by his almost ethereal appearance. Someone setting out to ignore him would have had ample excuse. His overall pallor – hair, face, even the old summer suit he wore – gave him a ghostly, unearthly look; created an impression of such transparency as to make his presence itself seem an illusion. I wondered for a minute whether Esmé really existed; whether I hadn't simply invented him. As if to reinforce this idea, Esmé fixed his gaze on me and, finally acknowledging that his entrance had no hope of recognition, came hobbling in my direction.

As he approached I realised how the woman at the hotel had made her mistake about his age. He looked even older than before; much older than the five-year gap accounted for. And much iller. All the same he managed his old dilapidated smile as he reached me.

'My God, it's a long way from that door!' he said. 'I'm actually *slower* than a snail. I tried to race one the other day. Outclassed all the way.' As he spoke, his face was a virtual pool of water. His eyes ran so much that the smallest movement caused tears to cascade down his cheeks. Saliva oozed from the corners of his mouth and he held a handkerchief to his nose almost constantly.

'You look like a runny egg, Esmé,' the Scottish girl said.

Esmé nodded, setting the stream in motion again. 'It's the mild Tangier climate,' he said. 'If I were down at Marrakesh you could fry me on the pavement.'

He laughed, which was tantamount to watching a cloudburst.

'What's happened to those plays of mine?' he suddenly asked me. 'I've heard nothing. Did you find somewhere suitable for them?'

I said I'd sent them to the National Theatre.

'They haven't replied. Unless those Février bastards haven't forwarded my letters.'

I said I'd enclosed his agent's address, as he'd instructed.

'Yes, but she died thirty years ago,' he said. 'I don't know who runs her place now. Probably never heard of me. Oh well. It doesn't matter now I'm writing verse again. D'you know any poetry publishers? I'll make some copies, if you like, and you can take them back. It's avant-garde stuff. No rhymes or anything like that.'

I thought Esmé seemed tense. He spoke more sharply than I remembered. When we discussed the Islamic revival, for instance, and I said the young here seemed too bound up in material goods to be very susceptible, he said shortly:

'I think you're wrong. It's the over-forties who were brought up under European rule who don't like this Islamic nonsense. The young teenagers are all for it. Students – that's to say, Communist types. They're plotting to get rid of the King.'

Islamic-loving Communists seemed a strange idea to me, for all the confusions (and fusions) of the modern world. I was going to raise the point but a servant appeared with a tray of drinks and Esmé took two. 'Saves time,' he said; then asked me to excuse him. 'I'm recruiting for *my* party tomorrow. I'm only asking *selected* people.' (Much of the party was spent talking about other parties. There was hot competition for the Forbes' Palace function this Saturday. Esmé hadn't been asked.)

As Esmé went, I heard a squawk of surprise to my left and turning found Mrs Spicer at my side. 'You've come back!' she said incredulously, as if this was a most unusual act among those who had met her. I said how nice it was to see her again and she roared with laughter, as always determined never to miss a joke by breaking into guffaws at everything you said. I told her I'd waved to her at her window the other day. 'But you didn't see me.' 'Oh, I never wave to anyone from my window,' said Mrs Spicer. 'You never know *what* people might expect!' She took a drink from a passing tray. She seemed in good form.

'You're at the Villa de France again, are you?' she asked. 'Such a pity it's gone off now the van der Meers have gone. They say the food's perfectly dreadful.'

'Always happens when Moroccans take over,' said the Scottish girl, who'd clearly picked up the local prejudices very quickly.

Mrs Spicer raised her head and gave a clap-of-thunder laugh. '*Moroccans?*' she exclaimed in amazement. 'It was bought by the Algerian who owns the Café de Paris. So much for *Moroccanisation!* Oh, it's all right so long as you're Arab,' she explained. 'Poor Mr van der Meer died, you know,' she continued, her expression changing from high comedy to deep mourning with all the speed of folding curtains closing on a stage. 'His wife soldiered on but it was too much for her. She's still here of course – you can't get money out of this country. They gave him a wonderful funeral. All the staff came. They carried the coffin on their shoulders. But within a month they were all stealing again,' she concluded with a sigh.

Her husband joined us. 'That appalling Brendon Brandon is here,' he said, adopting his square-legged stance.

'He's not Brendon Brandon, he's Brandon Brendon,' the Scottish girl said.

'Well, whatever he's called, he's drunk. And he started dancing with our Ahmed. Absolutely disgraceful.'

'It's up to Nina to do something,' said Mrs Spicer. 'It's her party.'

'Yes, but they're our servants.' Mr Spicer looked at me, squinting a little through his glasses.

'D'you remember this young man?' his wife asked him.

'Oh yes! Oh yes indeed!' said Spicer. He clearly had no idea who I was.

'Remember he came to lunch?' said Mrs Spicer. 'With his doctor friend.' She smiled charmingly at me.

'Oh yes! Oh my word yes!'

'How is England?' Mrs Spicer asked. 'We don't go there if we can help it.'

'England is coming along fine!' Mr Spicer replied, answering his wife's question so swiftly and naturally that for a second I thought I had myself uttered the words and wondered how I could have expressed so eccentric a viewpoint. 'Under Mrs Thatcher, England is set fair for the future.'

'You didn't think much of Mrs Thatcher when she closed the Consulate,' said Mrs Spicer.

Mr Spicer nodded gravely. 'I certainly never thought I'd live to see a Conservative government do that to us. But there it is!' he went on, swinging his drink in emphasis. 'We've all got to make sacrifices. I've just received a letter from a mill-owner friend of mine in Scotland and he says it's been hard, *very* hard. But he says it's the right thing and Mrs Thatcher must stick to it. It's the only way, he says. *Set fair for the future*, he says. Well, if I had the money I'd go back to England tomorrow.'

'I wouldn't to Scotland,' said the Scottish girl. 'My children would be hooligans!'

'Oh no!' Mr Spicer protested. He was genuinely alarmed.

'Oh yes!' the Scottish girl insisted. 'The schools are nothing short of riotous!'

'Surely it's not as bad as that, is it?' Mr Spicer looked at me for support.

I tried to sound hopeful, said no, but certainly many grammar schools had been closed or given a prominent rôle in the new enterprise culture.

'Oh *no*!' Mr Spicer was in despair. 'The Socialists have ruined the education system too!' He stared at me wild-eyed, almost pleading for some sign that this was an elaborate hoax.

I shook my head sadly, gave a parody of Nina's down-curling of the lip (I'd had a few drinks by this time). Mr Spicer frowned. Clearly his Francophobia was no better. Even this slightest of Gallic reminders was painful to him. But the Scottish girl went further.

'It's absolutely true!' she said. 'At home my children wouldn't learn half what they do here at the French School.'

Mr Spicer lowered his eyes. 'I can't believe *that*,' he said grimly.

The Scottish girl nodded her head vigorously. 'Yes! Yes! Really!' she repeated. 'They speak fluent French and Arabic.'

This was too much for Mr Spicer. 'What's the point of that?' he boomed, his face creased with exasperation, suggesting he was in physical pain. 'They're British, aren't they? What about their English?'

The Scottish girl pivoted her head in a so-so gesture. 'I admit we have a bit of trouble communicating at times,' she conceded quietly.

I asked – with a glance towards the Brandon Brendon show in the middle of the room – how the American School was.

'*Much* better,' said Mr Spicer, looking relieved at being on less desperate ground. (His heart is not good apparently.) '*He's* left, I'm glad to say.' (Pointing at the cavorting figure.)

'Disgraced?' I enquired.

'Oh no!' said Mr Spicer, a canny edge creeping into his tone. 'He's been appointed to the new Académie Marocaine!' He smiled in triumph.

'He's found his niche at last,' said Mrs Spicer.

Her husband nodded emphatically. 'Give them a taste of their own medicine,' he said with satisfaction.

Nina had appeared with Brigadier Hasta. Not remembering we knew each other, she introduced him to me; but as 'General'. (She was slightly tipsy by now.)

Hasta smiled. 'Nice to receive promotion at my age,' he said, 'but I'm afraid my superiors never had the confidence in me you seem to do.'

Mrs Spicer aimed a laugh at the ceiling. 'Oh, that's *nothing* new!' she said in a blasé tone. 'Nina always gets muddled about military men. Their rank, I mean,' she added subtly.

There was a silence. I heard again the strains of 'The Galloping Major'. Hasta, sensing trouble ahead but not knowing the lie of the land, launched a manoeuvre which, though designed to avoid the awkward terrain, actually drove us further into it. (Perhaps his superiors had been right about him.) 'Are you enjoying living over the Fez market?' he asked Nina.

An expression passed over Nina's face, with the speed and effect of a burst of sunshine suddenly illuminating a landscape, that had all the lofty scorn and yet perfect composure and poise of the most brilliant belle époque hostess. 'Why, *of* course!' she said. 'I *can't* tell you how absolutely enchanting it is to inhabit two tiny *little* rooms within smelling distance of *every* vegetable known *to* mankind! And *be*sides,' she added, piercing Mrs Spicer with a look of supreme contempt, 'it has for me so many charming *a*ssociations!'

Even Mr Spicer (to whom a French accent must be as pleasant a sound as flat top notes to a tenor) looked won over by this virtuoso command Nina's immersion in English culture gave her of irony, which he practised in a grim form himself but which his wife, who went in for innuendo, seemed to have no defence to. There is not much you can do when your victim acknowledges, even if by default, what you were only trying to imply.

'We live over a market ourselves – and it's delightful,' was all Mrs Spicer could manage. She turned instead to the Brigadier, saying how upset she was to hear he'd been bitten by his concierge's dog. 'I do hope it didn't draw blood,' she said with a glint in her eye.

'As a matter of fact, it did,' said the Brigadier. 'But luckily the trouser stopped it getting too deep. And the wretched woman swears she's had it inoculated against rabies. So that's all right. But I was absolutely furious! I like dogs,' he added, 'but I'm not a dog worshipper. Too many people are. Don't approve of it. They like it because they can have *power* over the animal.'

'Well, but isn't that better than *to* have power over people?' Nina said. 'As *in* the Army?' (She had perhaps not realised the accidental nature of his remark about her Fez market flat.)

Before Hasta could reply Mr Spicer mentioned some friend of his whose car had been stolen with his dog inside.

'He's worried more about the dog than the car. But I agree with him. Animals are our fellow creatures…'

I was afraid we were going to get his animal-hating-Christians-as-racists views again (cf. Spicers' lunch last time). But the mention of the stolen car instantly steered us into the never-distant region of muggings and burglaries.

'I've had new locks installed,' said the Brigadier.

'I've put broken glass and barbed wire on the walls,' said Mr Spicer.

'And bars on the windows,' his wife added.

'I left one window without them, for the view. And that's the one they came in through. So I've barred that up too.'

'*This* house is very vulnerable,' said Mrs Spicer. Perhaps mindful of her husband's heart, she thought a less personal review of the subject would be safer.

But Mr Spicer – model citizen – was no less passionate on the general behalf.

'It certainly is!' he agreed. 'Got old tiles, that's why. If I wanted to break into this house, I'd remove a few old tiles, then hole through the plaster – and you're in!'

'It's true,' said Mrs Spicer. 'I was having a cup of tea – ten past six in the morning it was (I like to be up early) – when I heard a noise and, would you believe it! – they were coming through the roof!'

All this was familiar enough. Sort of party talk you hear in Britain nowadays though here they see the atmosphere of siege as a local feature. So far the party had proceeded much as expected. Nothing had prepared me for what was to follow.

Spicer and the Brigadier had got talking about Rhodesia. Brigadier very shocked. 'All those years of sympathy from the Socialists and then betrayed by the Conservatives!' They were soon heading for the remoter reaches of reaction.

This left me alone with Nina and Mrs Spicer. It was as I was wondering how to keep the peace between them that the first untoward circumstance occurred. Rev. Jones entered arm-in-arm with a lavishly dressed blonde woman. I could hardly believe my eyes! I knew from our first trip that Tangier clerics were often louche to say the least, but had never suspected Rev. Jones of the faintest impropriety. Had he now gone the way of his notorious predecessors? And this so soon after the sumptuous episcopal nuptials with the lovely Miss Mare!

To my even greater astonishment the woman flounced floozy-like across the room and came straight up to me, saying:

'Well, hello! How are *you*? How *marvellous* to see you!'

My feeling of shock, coupled with the image of 'floozy' that had so readily come to mind, made me think perhaps I'd finally picked up the stiff Tangier manners. But then even in styleless old Britain now, I thought, you'd have trouble getting away with a come-on as brazen as this!

I made one or two non-committal comments, by which time Rev. Jones had caught up with his precocious companion. He greeted me, shook my hand, then stood fidgeting with his own, looking more chastened than straightforwardly embarrassed.

Meanwhile the blonde woman rabbited on, accompanying her remarks with a swaying motion that made the light catch her highly-polished handbag. It was not till I heard her reminisce about 'that *lovely* day we had – d'you remember? – at *Asilah*' that the terrible truth dawned: the woman before me was Miss Mare…

For the next few minutes I hardly took in a thing she said. I was wholly preoccupied with trying to extract from this new and brilliant creation the person I had met just a few years before, who had so impressed me with her ability to raise to fresh heights of attainment the English tradition of dowdiness.

The pancake make-up and dyed blonde hair were in themselves remarkable. But I stood near-mesmerised by the pink low-cut party frock, the high-heeled shoes she rocked backwards and forwards on, and that handbag she swung with such abandon. Here surely was proof of the continuing strength of the marriage bond!

It was lucky for me that we were almost at once joined by Miss Stray. Her stream of jokes gave me an excuse for the smirks and contortions to control them which Miss Mare must have been beginning to find inexplicable unless fashioned on her account. Then Esmé came back from his reconnoitre for party guests.

'It's going to be *very* select tomorrow,' he said. 'Because most of the people I'd selected can't come. "Can't" in inverted commas,' he observed, adding: 'Wish I hadn't asked them now.'

All this took some time to get out because, apart from his natural impediments, Esmé was juggling glass, stick and cigarette, puffing at the latter between phrases till its ash had lengthened to danger point and he stumbled slightly as he leant towards a passing servant's tray to deposit it. At the same moment Miss Stray, not wanting to miss this opportunity (her glass had been emptily jangling with ice for some seconds), reached out for a refill and the two arms collided.

'Whoops!' said Miss Stray. 'Our first physical contact for six years! Must drink to that!'

'You two really ought to make it up,' Rev. Jones said, his lilting voice bringing a natural note of regret to the suggestion. 'Forgive and forget after all.'

'But they *have* made it up!' his ebullient wife exclaimed, her handbag almost flying from her grasp. Her every utterance now was accompanied by a sweep of the hand or some other brilliant gesture. 'They've made it up just by being here together. Years since they were seen side by side in public.'

Neither of the two parties showed much sign of wanting to celebrate the event. The carousings of each were distinctly one-sided. Miss Stray just said: 'I'm off to Spain anyway.' Esmé attended to his streaming face with a handkerchief.

I still couldn't work out why Esmé had turned up, knowing Miss Stray would be there. The reason was not long in coming.

Meanwhile, as if responding to Miss Mare's joy at the reconciliation, Esmé said: 'What d'you think of our vicar's wife then? Isn't she simply—' (he rolled the 'r') '—ravishing? I adore that shade of *gold*.'

Miss Mare had no illusions about compliments from Esmé, or anyone else probably. 'A sailor from Gib asked me where I got my "wig",' she said disarmingly, giving one of her not exactly forced but unfunny laughs. 'Many people would've been offended. I wasn't. I just said it cost a fortune to get it this colour and I for one was very pleased with the result. Mind you, I wrote to his commanding officer to complain.'

Rev. Jones looked unhappy with the course the conversation was taking.

'Wonderful spread they've laid on this evening,' he said by way of diverting it.

His wife agreed. 'Yes,' she said, 'it's particularly good to see such a splendid supply of drink. Don't know where they can have got it from. So hard to come by now. Not that I'm much of one for it myself. But I naturally like to see others content.'

Miss Stray and Esmé remained silent; or as silent as their respective ablutions permitted. Miss Stray's were no more than a cursory flushing of the cistern but Esmé's by now were approaching emetic proportions. He was hardly capable of even a gesture without dislodging some current of water. More liquid seemed to flow into his glass than out of it.

'Have you had trouble getting alcohol here?' Miss Mare asked me. (Can't – for all her transformation – get into the habit of calling her Mrs Jones.)

I mentioned that we couldn't get wine in the fish restaurant at Asilah.

'That's new,' Miss Stray said glumly.

'There's still a Spanish-owned one you can get it at,' Esmé said knowledgeably. 'But it's bound to change hands.'

I explained how in Taroudant they made us hide our wine under the table, and even at the Mamounia in Marrakesh the waiter brought it glass by glass over acres of lounge because bottles could only be served in the restaurant.

Everyone began to look depressed. Rev. Jones took a gulp of his drink as if it might turn out to be the last.

Miss Mare – alone remaining buoyant – gave a meticulous account of the liquor laws (no alcohol in medinas, only glasses in cafés and bars, restrictions even in hotels) as if that would keep the conversation cheerful. In the present company, of course, it could not but have the reverse effect.

I thought it a bit sadistic of her to add:

'Anyway, I don't think wine *goes* with Moroccan food.'

('Who needs it to go with anything?' Miss Stray murmured in my ear.)

I pointed out that some Moroccans drank with or without food, and recounted the incident at the Parade.

'The man was quite right,' said Esmé. 'If we're to be persecuted for alcohol, why should the Moroccans themselves be allowed to drink it with impunity? I'm afraid I've become a disillusioned Arabist,' he added to me; 'you can't favour Arabs any more once you appreciate the appalling atrocities against the Jews.'

'I don't see what that's got to do with it,' Miss Mare said in a forthright tone. 'Besides,' she went on, 'hashish is illegal in the West, so why should Morocco make alcohol available?'

The régimiste flavour of this remark was too much for Miss Stray.

'Because they've got a damn good wine industry the French left them!' she said sharply. 'And their economy's not so hot they can afford to let it run down.'

'Quite,' said Esmé, adding: 'That would be an absurd case of sour grapes.'

Miss Stray gurgled into her latest gin. Miss Mare looked briefly at her beautifully shod feet, then – as if this simple gesture signified the transition to weightier topics – said:

'Isn't it good news that Anthony Crashaw is coming? Normally never goes to anything below Forbes' Palace level.'

But Miss Stray was not to be beaten.

'Only coming because his father knew Harvey Lambert's father,' she said. 'In MI5 together or something.'

'Is that so?' Rev. Jones seemed very interested. I recalled from the first trip his suspicions of Lambert on that score (not to mention the packages we'd taken back to London for him).

'Harvey was intended for the Diplomatic,' said Esmé. 'Learned French, Spanish, Arabic – God knows what. But it never came off.'

'I'd like to know how he can afford to keep this place going,' Miss Mare said soberly. I marvelled at how beneath her new lavish exterior her personality remained broadly unchanged.

'Well, how d'you afford *your* pile?' Miss Stray asked in a tone which, of anyone but her, you'd call dry. A momentary evaporation did seem to have taken place though. She was dry at least as gin is dry.

'I have an income,' Miss Mare said shortly. 'Whereas Harvey has no visible income. Apart from that little bit of teaching he does. It's very strange,' she concluded, giving the words a light, positive inflection, as if espousing the cause of human variety and the fruitful part played in it by Lambert's strangeness. (A cause though she would better have supported by not raising the income question in the first place.)

'He's a strange man, Harvey Lambert.' Rev. Jones made another attempt to steer the talk away from his wife's personal affairs. Her wealth was a particularly sensitive subject. It was in danger of placing him with his less reputable predecessor, something he'd done nothing – least of all his marriage to Miss Mare – to deserve. 'He turned up at church for the service of King Charles the Martyr,' he went on, of Lambert. 'Thought he was having me on.'

'Oh no,' Miss Mare said. 'He's in the Royalists. And the King Charles Brethren. You mustn't think he pulls the wool over our eyes just because he wears it over his own.'

'Can't help feeling a patch would be more stylish,' her husband reflected. 'Or even a glass eye.'

Esmé shook his head (which watered adjacent flowers).

'Mrs Févier used to say he couldn't have a glass eye because there's a cavity behind the lost one. She said he'd only half a brain.'

'Oh, that's absurd,' said Rev. Jones soberly (but taking another drink). 'She wasn't really with it at the end, was she?'

'I suppose not,' his wife said slowly. 'She always had a sharp tongue though…'

But all this was passing over my head, because just then I'd heard a name that made my heart miss a beat. Someone said: 'Oh look – the Hubert-Smythes are here.'

It was as if, like Chabrier at the performance of *Tristan,* I'd been waiting ten years to hear those sounds. I could concentrate on nothing else, only that name – Hubert-Smythe – and all it portended. It is after all *five* years since I first developed my craving to experience the Hubert-Smythean view of the world that so outrages everyone here. And throughout that first visit – and so far on this one – fate decreed that I should remain in the dark. Now I found myself at least in the same room as these beings. Surely this time I couldn't be frustrated.

I craned my neck to gain a glimpse of them without seeming to be distracted from the conversation of my group. The person who'd mentioned them – it was the Scottish girl as it happened – was looking in their direction. I followed her gaze and there they were: two nondescript, not to say dowdy, individuals. I had envisaged infinitely more striking figures. But the Scottish girl was hailing them, so there could be no mistake. The woman looked American, but in no other way distinctive; and her husband's appearance had nothing at all odd about it, his sole defect a strong resemblance to Lyndon B Johnson.

Though they had acknowledged the Scottish girl's wave, they showed no sign of coming over to join her. They were in an isolated part of the room, a little way from the door, and still too lately arrived to have made much progress from their opening position. I decided that Mohammed was going to have to go to the mountain if contact had a chance of being made.

At the first opportunity I set off, Miss Mare and Rev. Jones having drifted away, Miss Stray going after a drinks tray and Esmé feeling the need to sit down in a chair.

By this stage the party had become hectic; the atmosphere stagey, operatic even. Everyone was shouting to get over everyone else. Somehow the supply of drink was holding out, Mrs Spicer's servants still impeccably doling it to everyone. The contrast between their extreme sobriety and the raving intoxication of the guests (including the elegant Moroccan ones) meant that any style the event might pretend to was created entirely by those waiting on them. You could see how the native views on alcohol were constantly being reinforced.

Looking round, I could hardly believe that this was the same room that only an hour or two ago had housed Harvey Lambert and his world. Where was Lambert? Where, for that matter, was G? I'd last glimpsed him through the door standing by the staircase in heated conversation with the Scottish guy. Our eyes met briefly and he seemed to beckon anxiously. But Nina had steered me away and since then I'd seen nothing of him. Thinking he might be in the garden – and anyway feeling in need of fresh air by this time (it was stifling in the room) – I made that my target, deciding that even the Hubert-Smythes could wait till I was more compos mentis and had regained my partner – who I knew would relish the meeting as much as I would.

But it was quite difficult to cross the room, so many people were now grouped in the centre, and the servants constantly weaving around, balancing their trays, added to the congestion. Brandon Brendon was holding the stage again. He was screaming at the top of his voice that we should all get cholera, the water supply was so contaminated in Tangier. 'One can use mineral water for one's own ice, but what about other people's? That's what you've got to think of!'

'Just ask for wine,' said an American woman dressed in black silk who throughout had behaved as if she were at the most brilliant fin-de-siècle reception.

I was briefly detained by a big blond man whom I vaguely recognised from the Parade regulars. Nina had earlier introduced him to me as a man who'd had 'a very *full* life' (ran a bar that never closed). He was telling the man who'd been a journalist in Sweden that another European-owned restaurant had 'gone Moroccan'.

'It was famous for its hand-picked fruit,' the man who'd been a journalist in Sweden informed me.

'Also for its hand-picked boys,' said the man who'd run the bar that never closed.

'Apparently the hand-picked boys have taken over,' said the man who'd been a journalist in Sweden.

'Yes, they've grown into hand-picked criminals,' said the man who'd run the bar that never closed.

My first obstacle was the group round the Spicers. I didn't want to get dragged again into that particular fantasy world. They were hogging the Chief of Police, a small neat man just arrived who kept saying 'We *want* Europeans here.' Mr Spicer (who'd told me before how anti-European the Moroccan authorities were becoming) nodded in agreement and, pointing at the Police Chief, remarked to his neighbour: 'Useful man to know.' This, like the earlier talk of robberies, had a familiar ring to it from home.

I then bumped into the honeymoon couple from the hotel. They looked at their wits' end. They had taken shelter in a corner of the room as if expecting violent onslaught at any moment. 'The Colony here is very lively!' the woman said bravely. 'I was in India,' said her husband. 'But never anything like this.'

I had reached the doors opening onto the garden and was in sight of refuge when somebody grabbed my arm and my heart sank at the prospect of more human contact. I turned in despair and had made a reflex shaking-off motion before waves of relief rushed over me as I took in the smiling face of G.

'Thank God it's you,' I said. 'Can't take much more.'

'No. Me neither. Just had a weird tale from that Scottish guy about acoustic neuroma.'

'About *what?*'

'Acoustic neuroma. You know, inoperable. Fatal. Tell you the details later. Six months to live – gave up everything – came out here. Final fling etc. All turned out to be a mistake.'

'How very convenient.'

'That's what I thought. Listen – the Hubert-Smythes have invited us for a drink at their place.'

'*They have?*'

(Had he told me we were invited to a reception for the Second Coming I couldn't have shown greater interest. This is the level of absurdity the writer's instinctive curiosity can bring you to.)

But even that hysterical response of mine was overtaken by what happened next.

(Now 11 a.m. as I write. *Esmé's* party is at noon. So must get this down first. But will it take place after what happened last night? No time to think. Back to the plot.)

G – who had made his farewells – went off through the garden to join the Hubert-Smythes. I said I'd make mine and meet him and them at the front of the house in about ten minutes.

I had just started heading towards Nina – who by now was having almost physically to restrain Brandon Brendon – when a hush came over the room so sudden and dramatic after the previous hubbub that I really thought I'd gone deaf. I had no time to reflect on it, though, because the eyes of all were turned on the door and following the general gaze I saw that the Hon. Anthony Crashaw had arrived.

He came in wearing a three-piece tropical suit (though the evening was dank and it had just started raining), walking with a soft, almost prancing step which gave his movements not so much an affected as slow-motion quality, as if to prolong the entrance without appearing to. Jerkily he shifted his head from side to side as his smile was bestowed all around. He held his hands clasped in front as though permanently shaking them with himself. In all other respects though his manner was just that of the average débutante.

On the previous occasions I'd seen him – always briefly – I wondered if he was sending himself up, or at any rate his absurdly inflated reputation. It was this parodic air about him that modified what in another man of his age and sadly shrivelled looks would have been grotesque in the extreme. I recalled the remark attributed to him (forget by whom) about people coming here social-climbing and finding only 'screaming old him' at the top of the tree.

But from this longer and fuller sight I realised the self-parody was really an act of self-defence against the charge of conceit it was meant to conceal. This became clear to me now as he paraded round the room – a model exhibiting clothes at a fashion show (there was even a smattering of applause) – a wave here and there – a 'Hi!' or 'Hel*lo*!' (mouthed not voiced) before, his initial circuit completed, people began talking again, more subdued though than before. A superbly crafted performance, a perfect study in the subtle art of feigned self-deprecation. I remembered the actor Max Adrian's habit of pushing his hands through the air, as if warding off the audience applause.

As I started to cross the room – clearer since Crashaw's tour of inspection and the preferable route now the rain was coming down quite hard in the garden – I noticed Esmé stretched out asleep in his chair, looking terrible. I was about to pause and see if he needed help when he woke and almost at once leapt up – with a speed and suddenness in themselves extraordinary but made all the more so by the contortions that accompanied them. Half-stumbling, stick extended in front of him, he made his way across the floor towards Crashaw, who had his back to him, covering the ground – some five or six feet – with a swiftness that had seemed impossible earlier.

Crashaw stood addressing a couple of the elegant Moroccans. 'You must come up,' he was saying. 'Give me a ring—' Then turning to move on – the Chief of Police had hailed him with a beaming smile – he virtually collided with Esmé, who seemed to think Crashaw was about to leave – he must have been asleep for his arrival (and he'd told me before that Crashaw was always 'last to come, first to go').

The desperation in Esmé's manner made Crashaw raise a hand in self-defence (Esmé for all his dereliction is the taller). This, breaking the clasped arrangement – which took in the holding of his drink – left one hand dangling adrift, upsetting both his poise and his glass. The wine splashed more on him and the elegant Moroccans than on Esmé – for whom extra moisture would have been no great hardship. A servant sped to Crashaw's assistance but Esmé ignored the ministrations and said:

'Lovely to see you here, Anthony! As it happens, I came specially on your account—'

Though as usual he spoke slowly and with immense over-enunciation, somehow the words seemed to come out in a rush, like a prepared speech – so much so that after these I heard no more till the final staccato phrase: 'I-want-ed-to-in-vite-you-to-my-par-ty.'

The room had gone quiet again. Everyone, drawn by the spilling of the drink, went on looking that way. The two men stood blankly facing one another, like duellists about to turn and measure out their paces: Esmé quivering, barely able to stand upright; Crashaw by contrast at attention – his glass had been removed and he held his hands stiffly by his side as if, now the clasp had failed, this was the only place for them.

'Thank you... Thank you very much...' he murmured. Then, his smile crumpled but undislodged: 'When is the function to take place?'

'Tomorrow. Tomorrow at noon.'

'I see. Rather short notice—'

'Yes.'

'May I ask where?'

'At my abode in the Pension Buonavita. Rue de la Plage. On the roof if fine.'

Crashaw looked round as if for support, as if some devastating event – collapse of ceiling or near-equivalent – had occurred. Then, very quietly, and in the kindest of tones, he said:

'I'm afraid I couldn't... I couldn't possibly...'

Time stopped. No one moved or made a sound. A canvas appeared before me with the caption: *The Hon. Anthony Crashaw Cuts Mr Esmé St Clair at a Reception. Tangier 198–.*

Esmé bore an expression of agony so intense his features seemed about to come apart. But oddly his face, so tearful in appearance, had lost its watery look; if anything, the skin now seemed parched, arid, stiffened even. He barely had the strength to come out with his exit line – 'You bastard! You self-satisfied bastard!' – and stagger towards the door. He would certainly have fallen to the floor but for Miss Stray who came to him, put her arm round his waist and to the astonishment of all escorted him out of the room, the two old enemies tottering side by side in a version of a run-down double act.

(3 May)

Writing now – two days later – it seems astonishing to me that none of us saw then what we all now know: that Esmé had had a stroke.

Well, I'm not a doctor – though the bits and pieces I've picked up from G ought really to have told me. What undoubtedly should have struck me at once, if I have any powers of observation at all – was that Esmé had stage-managed that whole scene with Crashaw.

At the time I stood like most people rooted to the spot, less in shock than a disbelief I now see was justified. But I was too swept up in it all to trust my instinct; and preoccupied with meeting the Hubert-Smythes at last.

In retrospect that whole evening seems more like a night and a half. Yet Nina's party ('security conscious') was due to end at eight, and it was earlier than that when I left after the Esmé incident, feeling bewildered myself as I stumbled back through those cluttered and tomb-like rooms of Harvey Lambert's house (had seen nothing more of him – for reasons which will appear). Anyhow, it can barely have been ten when the Hubert-Smythes insisted on running us back to the hotel ('dark wet night – have to be careful') and I began the task of trying to write it all up.

But it could have been ten the next morning from the way I felt – and things haven't let up since: this is the first chance I've had to take up the story.

Ironically I was kept going by my eagerness to resolve the Hubert-Smythe question – which was exactly what prevented me seeing the full significance of the Esmé affair. Of which more later.

First then: they are *not* 'the Hubert-Smythes'. *He* is Hubert Smythe; *she* is Dorothy Smythe. So they are 'the Smythes'. Tangier (or American?) custom has transformed them. (This reminds me that the Spicers, according to Miss Stray, were once the Spenser-Spicers. Mrs Spicer added her maiden name – from motives of pure snobbery, with no thought of striking a blow for the feminist cause she abhors. But the tongue-twisting alliteration of the form was too much for decaying Tangiero lips and Mrs

Spicer quickly dropped it, preferring to forego her pretensions rather than live with absurdity.)

The Smythes' elegant villa (has 'The View') they acquired from the previous Spanish owner, against the tide of Moroccan ownership (Smythe: 'A tricky deal but a clean one'). It is surrounded by rubble. Some local councillor building himself a house. 'Out of public funds, of course,' said Smythe. 'Still, means extra security for us. Though we'd need more in Chicago or Cleveland.'

This remark itself made an impression on me. It was the first time here I could recall anyone showing awareness of present realities, of the world outside. (Significant that the Smythes go back to America two months each year.)

Inside the villa: pleasant American homely. No sign of the 'liveried flunkeys' Bidfine spoke of last time. (Incidentally have finally got through to him today: fixed a date – so must get all *this* down first.)

The Smythes hospitable in the American way. Sat us down, made us welcome, plied the drink. But now I was at last face-to-face with the man whose political views had kept me so long in suspense, an odd thing happened. I was reduced to silence.

Of course, I longed to get on to the subject – the quicker the better. I even deliberately withheld news of the Esmé incident, which they and G had not witnessed, so as not to get distracted. (This landed me in embarrassment next day when they learned of it and clearly couldn't understand how someone who'd seen the whole thing had failed to inform them ten minutes later. Unable to come clean – 'I was so desperate to hear your insane political views' – I was reduced to feeble remarks like 'Slipped my mind'. 'Slipped?' said Smythe. 'Sounds like wholesale collapse!')

But, as always when you're intent on raising something, I became hopelessly self-conscious. My normal instinct for conversation – need for subtle approaches and gentle beginnings –completely deserted me. The forms that came to me were crude beyond belief. 'I understand you have some interesting views on politics…' 'The political situation looks rather tense, don't you think?'

I felt like a phrase book, full of useless expressions, inconsequential tags doomed to be met with a look of total incomprehension, if not outright hostility.

I decided the only course was to let the talk drift naturally when sooner or later it was bound to skirt the subject our host was so keen on. Politics is never far from any conversation. Usual problem is keeping it out. I was about to discover the exception to the rule.

We talked about everything: the problems of maritime transportation, the future of newsprint, the state of contemporary dance. At times we touched shores that made even Harvey Lambert's seem positively adjacent. The one place we never managed to call at was the only one I wanted to go to.

I began to think that, like the Dutch-Australian at the hotel, Smythe was being purposely cagey, aware of the consequences of too open talk on a sensitive topic. But his reputation was for just such open discussion; more than that, he was supposed to be outrageous. So why should he clam up like this?

Then it dawned on me: it was exactly because of his reputation. Smythe was making a point of not living up to it. He was not going to be the quirky political bore they all made him out to be. He would refute the general view and at least send a couple of people away with a different impression. For the first time in my life I was longing for someone to be a bore. And for the first time I could remember, it wasn't going to happen.

Seeing Smythe's intention made it no easier for me to frustrate it. How *do* you make a man fall in with the stereotyped view of himself that he hates?

As usual in circumstances like these (cf. first meeting with the Waughs) it was G who made the breakthrough. (Is it diagnostic brilliance or more a knack with the social scalpel?)

For the twentieth time we were admiring 'The View'. And for the twentieth time Smythe was saying what could and could not be seen from their side of it. You could see Tarifa. And the Sierra. On a clear day, you could even see Cadiz. 'Not Gib though,' he repeated, but this time adding: 'Gib's too far to the right here.'

'As far to the right as the politics?' G – quick as a flash – put in. 'In that respect, most people seem a long way past Malaga.'

It was the key. Or rather it broke open the door by putting all the weight of quirky opinion on the other side. It offered Smythe a chance he could not let pass of a sympathetic audience. He came clean.

And?

I listened in amazement. I could not believe it.

I was hearing my own point of view!

I sat immobile, expressionless, spellbound. Trying to work it out.

I was seriously alarmed.

Had I misunderstood? Had I failed to spot the baldest irony, the most undisguised leg-pulling, in all the mystique that surrounded this man and his views? Or had my own views become so warped that I could no longer perceive their eccentricity?

Because otherwise I just could not see what all the fuss over Smythe was about. Viz.:

Style of speaking: relaxed, witty, trenchant but never overbearing.

History: consular, long since retired (CIA connection only during war). Very much the outsider.

General outlook: liberal, enlightened, not very hopeful. Straightforward pessimistic view of the world. Extremely sound.

Only now, having thought about it, do I realise that this was just another example of how in the face of orthodoxy (which the West's beloved 'pluralism' presents in a multitude of guises) perfectly sensible views appear eccentric, misguided, even mad, solely because they are at odds with received opinion. They don't even have to be specially brilliant or revelatory to seem so: by comparison with the general conservative blandness anything will appear outrageous. This certainly accounts for Hubert Smythe's position here: his views quite free of the subjectivity and self-interest that inform virtually everyone else's. Also – I couldn't help feeling, though it gives me small comfort (quite the reverse: makes me balk at the prospect), it helps explain my own increasing sense of isolation at home. As Smythe put it: 'This is the price you pay for buying nothing.'

After all my expectation I should have felt deflated by the way things turned out on the Hubert Smythe account. But any sense of anti-climax on this score was more than made up by the outcome of the Esmé affair.

In view of the previous evening's events, I was prepared for Esmé's party to be called off – irrespective of his stroke, which I didn't yet know about. But when we got to the Pension Buonavita (well after the noon starting-time: I'd been writing up *Nina*'s party till then), we were shown into the kitchen at the back – it was raining so the roof-top was out – and found about a dozen people nonchalantly helping themselves from a spread of food on the table.

They had all been at Nina's party – including some who'd turned down Esmé's invitation then; presumably turning up now in the failure of anything more alluring to materialise.

Esmé himself was not present. I asked Nina (who to my amazement was) where he'd got to. Given the thing was going ahead as arranged his absence seemed odd.

'He is not *very* well. He is in bed,' Nina told me. 'But hardly *sur*prising, I suppose.'

This veiled reference to Esmé's condition – assumed to have an alcoholic basis – was the closest she or anyone else came to mentioning the night before. All behaved as if nothing had happened. Brandon Brendon apologised to Nina for having been 'hopelessly drunk' at her party – which was like saying sorry for spilling water in a room newly flooded: even his antics had been completely upstaged by the Esmé-Crashaw scene. Besides, he looked and acted just the same now (and today we saw him cavorting round the garden of the Parade barely able to stand).

So everyone ate and drank and said what a pity it was that Esmé was 'indisposed'. That, as it turned out, was putting it mildly – and better described the state of the guests (ourselves included: 'last drinks' – as they termed it – with the Smythes had been fairly heavy).

G and I were debating whether or not to go up and see Esmé in his room when he finally appeared – carried in by the Spanish couple who still run the Pension Buonavita.

He wore a white silk dressing gown and a cigarette holder protruded lopsidedly from a corner of his mouth. G took one look and knew the worst. It was then too that I first got a glimmering of what I'd overlooked at the time. When, despite the calamity of the stroke, Esmé now played perfect host, asking if everyone had enough to eat and so on, it was clear as day the man had far too much style and savoir faire to approach Crashaw of all people as he had without some preconceived purpose. And the idea that the stroke – which must have occurred just before, while he was stretched out in the chair – made him behave so out of character is less convincing than the evidence of the stroke itself for his determination, even after it, to go ahead with his plan; a plan to humiliate Crashaw. Because it did humiliate him more than Esmé.

To people like Crashaw the mere mention of so preposterous an invitation ('on the roof if fine') is humiliating, since it exposes them to just the kind of scene their infallible taste and exclusiveness are meant to preserve them from. Crashaw was forced to drop his act of gracious condescension and publicly reveal his snobbishness and conceit.

Well, it certainly had that effect on me. But I don't need persuading. From the general point of view I suspect the plan (like Esmé's life as a whole) backfired. The ironies were probably beyond most people there. And the greatest irony – the accident of the stroke, which should have induced sympathy – went for nothing, just confirming the belief of everyone that Esmé was paralytic only in the drunken sense. We should of course have realised his condition had more than an alcoholic – or even emotional – cause. (Had G been present he would instantly have realised it – as he did when he saw Esmé next day.) Instead we all stood there gaping, imagining we watched the time-honoured spectacle of someone leaving a party incapable; not one of us with the nous to see what had really happened to the poor man.

Esmé though seemed much cheered at this sign that he might be on the way out. Adamantly refused G's suggestion that he go into hospital. (He described the Spanish Hospital here as the last outpost of the Inquisition.) 'Besides, the only treatment for anything is champagne,' he said. 'Champagne and *thin* chicken sandwiches.' Then, looking at the spread on the table: 'Well, at least we have the thin chicken sandwiches.'

He joked all the time, telling us to treat the party as his parting – a dummy run for his funeral breakfast ('with the accent on the dummy: they've invited the corpse by mistake'). He said you soon came to adopt the Arab view of death living here. 'Too many people spend their time saving those of us who're at death's door, when all we want them to do is open it for us. Might have managed it myself last night but for Stray here. Still, looks like nature's going to succeed where art failed.'

It was then that the full extent of Esmé's design became clear. He'd planned to take an overdose. Had the tablets with him at Nina's party, which – being well supplied with the required alcohol he'd have trouble getting alone – he saw as his best opportunity. The 'selected' guests for his party next day would turn up to find him dead: very dramatic. The scene with Crashaw would provide his grand exit. Hence his desperation to get to him when he woke and thought the tablets were starting to work – attributing to them the effect of the stroke he'd had instead: which had actually prevented him taking them.

This explains too, I think, the terrible look of anguish on his face as he went out with Miss Stray. He knew he'd failed again.

Any chance of carrying out his intention afterwards was foiled by Miss Stray who drove him back in Nina's car and stayed with him through the night, suspecting the worst.

At his party, Esmé and she went to great lengths to revive their old enmity, unable to bear being thought sentimental.

'Sheer force of habit,' Miss Stray told us re her rescue act. 'Did nursing in the war.'

'The way you drove Nina's car we should both have perished in any case.'

'Darling, I haven't driven a car for at least twice the time we haven't been speaking. Besides, I'm used to driving trucks. It's a different technique. They get out of your way.'

'We both slobber, as you know,' Esmé said. 'But even that isn't as disgusting as slobbering over each other as we were all last night.' Then to Nina: 'Some people seem to think I ruined your party. Others, that I made it. Which view do you subscribe to?'

Nina turned down a lip. 'Well, but it *hard*ly matters. Anthony Crashaw came *en*tirely on Harvey Lambert's account, and now Harvey *has* been arrested.'

'*Arrested?*' We all chorused the word.

'Oh yes. But *did*n't you know?'

(The sang froid of this was a bit forced. Had too much cold-bloodedness about it.)

'The whole thing is of course quite *ri*diculous. They see Harvey living in this *ma*gnificent house without visible means of support, so they are ab*so*lutely convinced he is spying for someone. Last night they send the Chief *of* Police to distract us while all his officers were searching *the* house!'

'Of course,' Miss Stray put in, 'our dear vicar's wife was also baffled about Harvey's wherewithal…'

'And the Spicers are great friends of the Chief of Police,' Esmé added.

Both sipped their drinks as if the dryness of these remarks needed moisture for their implications to sink in.

'Well, but *in* any case,' said Nina, 'as they have found ab*so*lutely nothing – except Esmé's tablets strewn *a*cross a table – I don't see *what* they think they *can* do.'

'After interrogating Harvey, they'll be too exhausted to do anything,' said Miss Stray. 'Harvey doesn't withhold information. He dispenses it. By the time he's finished with them, they'll be the most knowledgeable policemen in Tangier. They'll have the lowdown on every underworld figure from pre-history to 5th-century Athens.'

'I expect some Arab wants his house,' said Esmé. 'A bribe in the right quarter and they put on the pressure. Encourages you to sell. This is the advantage of being a clapped-out poverty-stricken wreck like me. It's the one nasty thing that can't happen to you.'

'There are so many nas*ty* things,' Nina reflected. Then, with an uncharacteristically crude shrug of hopelessness: 'Well, but this is *Tan*ger now.'

I suppose that sums it up. But in the artificial verve of her party, in its forced and reckless energy, and above everything else in the desperation of Mrs Spicer's constant and undiscriminating laughter – as if to stop for a second would let in unthinkable thoughts – it was strangely the mood of contemporary Britain that kept coming to mind.

4 May

Our last full day. An odd morning. Swirling mist over the Straits. 'The View' very English. (It's today we're having lunch with Tommy Bidfine.)

Writing over breakfast in the Petit Socco (the hotel swarming with the French-speaking coach party. Who are actually Belgian).

Hubert Smythe told us that thirty years ago you could come here at 4 a.m. and find it livelier than it is now at midday. In those days, he said, the Parade was 'very wild'. It belonged to two Americans who died of drink. He recalled a couple from Marseilles who sang the most obscene songs he'd ever heard. They died of drink. A young British peer ran the best beach bar in Tangier. (He *came* here to die of drink.) 'Yes, those were the days, they all say,' said Hubert Smythe.

Sitting here now, I can imagine the kind of conversation that must have gone on as the changes set in. First, a casual remark or two (*'Have you noticed…? Did you hear…?'*). Then a phase of joking about it (*'Saw so-and-so staggering along dead sober – said he couldn't get a drink in the Socco'*). Gradually more and more talk of problems, signs of the times, departures (*'…had a break-in…' 'this new law…' 'X has gone. Y says he's going…'*). Finally the truth has to be faced: the game is up. This is no great feat of imagination. We've been through it all in Britain. But in Britain we can – and do – pretend. Our camouflage is greater. Here there are too many reminders of the truth (Miss Stray: 'Difficult to pretend when you're being kicked out on your arse.')

'A privileged breed in decline is generally better than one in the ascendant,' said Hubert Smythe. 'People become nicer when the chips are down. But that's just when they get chucked out, so it's a futile way of thinking. The whole history of Morocco just about sums it up. Whenever anyone gets civilised, they get ousted by a new bunch of barbarians – and usually rich ones – who of course will go the same way when they acquire better manners. Civilisation is an individual thing. You teach yourself, whereas societies work by numbers. So they never stay civilised for long.'

He doesn't rate Hassan's chances highly here. Sees him – in a decade, perhaps less – going into exile; possibly even an Islamic 'revolution'. 'If it does come it'll be the kids growing up now who'll lead it. They'll be the ones to react against all the industrial crap. Much as kids did in the West. Only here it means something. But – Hassan may play his cards right. Being religious as well as political head, he's got one that the Shah never had. 'Stead of rejecting religion as out-of-date and liable to hold up material progress, you make it part and parcel so to speak. Like we've done with Christianity. Use it to bolster things up. Means you let in Western influence in the guise of respectable fellow-Islamic-loving, but fully Westernised Middle Easterners, taking over from the old colonial Europeans. Could work. On the other hand,' he went on, 'could cause resentment all round; from the anti-religious, who're opposed to Islam altogether, and from the super-devout who don't like seeing it put to secular use. You could end up with the worst of both worlds. You generally do. Beauty of it is that at the moment everyone here wants all the things we've all gotten disillusioned with. But, being like most so-called civilisations, totally unprincipled, we'll sell 'em all that junk so's to keep ourselves in clover. *And* the weapons to go with it, should they feel like blowing up anyone who's the leastways bit different from them. Still,' he concluded, replenishing our glasses with a springiness that belies his eighty-odd years, 'we must continue to pursue ideals – by which I don't of course mean the political and material goals with which the word is now thought to be synonymous. I mean the perfectly obvious fact that life should and could be wonderful for everyone. Which, being the simplest thing in the world to achieve, is the one thing no one can be bothered with. There's no money in it.'

On which note, off now to Nettlewood.

(8 p.m.)

The house loomed grey and mysterious in the mist that had cleared in Tangier but still clung round the Mountain as we drove up. The thought of describing our visit is daunting. But here goes.

Bidfine *very* pleased to see us, though full of mock-complaint. 'They say they're friends of mine,' he began, addressing an imaginary audience, 'yet they don't come near me till they're about to disappear!'

I explained how we'd rung several times (he's just got back

from South Africa); also that we'd expected to see him at Nina's party. 'Oh, I don't go to that kind of thing any more,' he said. (He'd not heard about Esmé's stroke. 'Ah so?' was his comment when I told him.)

But there was no doubt of his pleasure at seeing us again. He told us we looked younger and slimmer. The 'slimmer' may well be true, after all those half-eaten meals in the south. The 'younger' I was less sure of: I thought that, like him, I looked and felt five years older. (I noticed he walked a little stiffly.)

'So – you have seen tout Maroc,' he said as we came straight in to lunch. 'You went right down to the desert! Did you see the Great Bustard? Did I tell you I'm a bit of a bird fancier? I looked all over Europe for it at one time and d'you know where I finally saw it? Here in Morocco – hopping happily across the stony desert at Rissani!'

I was a little surprised that we were to eat immediately ('Mustn't keep the servants waiting!'), but could scarcely believe my ears when, as we entered the house, Bidfine said: 'You come on an historic day. Because today *Tel-e-vision* has come to Nettlewood! There's the aerial – see?'

Both of us must have shown our amazement because he instantly continued: 'Yes, but only for servants. Television is for servants and so it has been installed in servants' quarters.'

This turned out to be the least of the surprises in store. But I mustn't anticipate. At first we were quite unaware of the changes that had taken place. And certainly in the early stages Bidfine himself was much as before. He told us the 'make me chaste, Lord – but not yet' story as if it were unknown (attributing it to St Augustine) and showed us a picture of himself meeting the Queen in Rabat during the royal tour.

'She said, "There seem to be a lot of you from Tangier." "Yes, ma'am," I replied. "We're the *retired* people – as opposed to the *commercial* people here." I thought she'd appreciate that!' Also said how funny the Duke of Edinburgh had been when shaking hands ('"Absurd ritual this, isn't it?" he said. "Good thing we don't go in for rubbing noses." We had a good laugh together!')

All this was wildly in character. And as before interspersed with the occasional worldly 'I know' or 'Yes, but what can one do?'

which he affects, giving a sad smile of resignation, at any mention of the state of things here or at home; a habit that modifies his more outrageous views and helps to endear him to you.

As for the house, despite the fog it looked brighter and smarter than before, having just been redecorated (which accounted for a wet clay smell, similar to that at Lambert's house – where I think though it was more decay than decoration).

'We have a lovely cockney boy here who saves all our houses falling down,' Bidfine told us at lunch. 'I say "boy", he's actually in his forties. Well, that's young for Tangier. Heavens, *I*'m young for Tangier! He's been here fourteen years. Came out with a wealthy, elderly gentleman when his looks were, so to speak, his fortune... Decided to stay. Started his business. Very successful. Now lives up here. (On the *other* side, of course.) How he does it I couldn't say. Hasn't a word of Arabic but they all understand him – he works alongside them, very hard too. He deserves his success. Without being patronising, it is remarkable, I think, for a cockney boy with no education. Have some camembert – it's just right.'

. Lunch was good ('Our fare is Spartan but then the Spartans had good figures') and served by Mustafa's wife, Fatima. On the surface life at Nettlewood seemed unchanged but I began to sense that all was not well.

At first I was inclined to put this down to the swirling mist outside which gave the whole place an air of impending doom. The view was entirely obliterated and beyond the murky outline of the palms, which was all that was visible of the garden, a grey void stretched away to what might have been the end of the world.

But quite apart from fanciful ideas of this kind, I found cause for doubt in Bidfine's excessive well-being. Such total absence of complaint could mean only one thing: something was seriously wrong.

He spoke of the trip to South Africa from which he'd just returned. 'An *unqualified* success. Hadn't been for twenty-five years. Forgotten how really lovely it is. Absolutely perfect – except for a hideous journey back, caused by a strike at Lisbon. Hence the unanswered telephone.' (Hence? What about the servants? More anon – because Bidfine had swept on before I could intervene.)

'I was forced to go to England instead. Always an unpleasant business. As you will know. *Rar*lly, how do you put up with it? First I had to stay at one of those ghastly overpriced hotels, with the usual slovenly service. Then next morning at Heathrow I was in the usual enormous queue for what they call "refreshments" – i.e. a stale roll and the cup of gruel they insist is coffee – when suddenly the *entire* airport was empty! I and my suitcase alone remained! "Oh, it's only a bomb scare," they said at the counter. *Only*! Mind you, I felt infinitely safer sitting in the airport than scampering around with the loutish panic-stricken people on the runways! But, as if I needed any further dissuasion the whole experience determined me to keep off that terrible alcoholic island! Every time I go there it reminds me more and more of Russia where everyone gets drunk and plays chess all the time. Except in England they don't play the chess.'

From the material point of view things 'couldn't be better! I went to South Africa on business as well as pleasure – and made a lot of money! *Rar*lly, it's too dreadful! I get richer and richer while everyone else gets poorer and poorer! Soon no one will be able to afford holidays except me and I shall have all the Continental roads to myself again as one did once and drive happily round the lovely land of France that the French so richly *don't* deserve. You poor things,' he went on, 'you've been all over Morocco where now there are none of those charming little French-owned hotels I recall from my youth. All gone! Everything big and fit for the tourist herd. All is for the tourist herd. No one cares any more about the individual traveller. I've always been a traveller, never a tourist,' he concluded, adopting his look of sublime resignation. (I wondered if it occurred to him that his investments might well be spurring on the tourist herd at the expense of the individual traveller.)

But the first hint Tommy Bidfine gave to confirm my suspicions was by default. 'Yes, I get richer and richer,' he mused sadly. 'People say it's not fair. But then life isn't fair, is it? Once I was poor, now I am rich. Was it fair that I was poor? Is it any more fair that I am rich? Because this house alone is worth a fortune. I have offers – you know the Moors are buying property now. They too are making money and putting it into a valuable commodity. That is all they are interested in. You see, it comes to us all! And, like me, they are succeeding. I don't know how, but they are. Whenever a place comes up, it falls to the Moors as Spain and half the civilised world did once. That is why the Europeans are diminishing. But don't mistake me. For all the offers *I* shan't leave!' He smiled and sipped his coffee (we were in the study by now). 'Oh, I don't fall into the trap of moving because things aren't quite right. I've known people who've lived in Italy, the West Indies – everywhere. There's always some drawback. No, I shan't move from here,' he said emphatically, but in his anxiety to exclude the possibility neglecting to see that the true significance lay in its being raised at all. It implied that, however resistant he might be to leaving, circumstances now existed that made him at least contemplate the prospect, if only to reject it. This became clear almost at once, because he went on:

'But there are apparently those who are mad – or perhaps malicious – enough to think the opposite.'

He then described how he had received a visit from the Chief of Police who had – from what source he would not reveal to Bidfine – been informed he was involved in a sale of the house, the proceeds from which were to be deposited in Switzerland. (I thought it tactful not to mention the Harvey Lambert saga and the fact that the Chief of Police dined often at the Spicers'.)

'The man was impertinent enough to remind me that money cannot be taken out of Morocco. Of course, I was able to reply that, even without my absolute determination never to part with Nettlewood, I was in no need of extra-territorial funds such as its sale would provide. Should Morocco collapse, I should probably be in a far more secure position than that Chief of Police, since, although I can quite legally remove from South Africa all the money I've made there, I shall not do so as a precaution against that very contingency! And should you – as I suspect you are, because you are both such very *bright* boys – be wondering what happens if South Africa collapses, I will anticipate by explaining that, though the aforementioned Switzerland will not be further enriched by the sale of Nettlewood, it already harbours the bulk of my dear old fortune!'

He laughed quietly for a few moments, then raising his eyes to heaven, added: 'And if Switzerland collapses, well then, we are *all* dead men!'

Though I don't agree with it, I have to admire the completeness of Bidfine's view of the world, and the thoroughness with which he follows it through. Yet even this modest account of encroaching problems was less remarkable for what it revealed than for what it suggested – at least to me – lay still hidden. The manner in which all this gradually came out was fully confessional but Bidfine's poise and cunning were too great not to imbue it with a subtlety that wholly concealed the fact.

So when it was nearing five o'clock and we, wanting to be model guests and give our host the chance of getting rid of us, thanked him for lunch but said we mustn't take up any more of his time, Bidfine used the opportunity to disclose two crucial developments in life at Nettlewood under cover of a mock-rebuke to us for 'rushing off ungratefully'.

'Heavens!' he began, invoking the imaginary audience again; 'One hasn't seen them for years and they run away at the first occasion! And yet they know that a poor old gentleman like me living up here all alone hardly sees a soul to speak to! Not that there's many one *wishes* to speak to,' he added in a supposed aside to us, 'with what stimulating company there was vanishing at a rate of knots to other, stabler places, or else – what has to be faced at this stage of life – to the nether regions themselves. As for the remainder—' (he sighed deeply and raised his arms in a forlorn gesture) '—they don't read a book or do anything but play bridge and gossip. It's perfectly frightful!'

(As he said this, I had a sudden flash of memory: of that day on the first trip when Mrs Spicer came to the hotel and spoke of 'light reading' in such a way that G confused it with concern for excess baggage. Seems he was closer to the truth than he thought in seeing books here as an encumbrance. And now there is no consular library and the Librairie des Colonnes is Moroccan-owned...)

'However,' Bidfine had continued, 'I shan't bore you with all that, but ring for tea instead, so that we can take advantage of *this* opportunity for intelligent conversation – unless of course,' he added casually, 'you need a taxi – which, having your own transport this time, you don't. Luckily for you. Because taxis are now hors de combat up here after dark. Yes!' he affirmed, seeing our sceptical looks; 'Because as so often in this far from ideal world, when one comes to a rich residential area like this, one has first to traverse a humbler zone of habitation.'

I nodded; I remembered the area well. It was where the waiter from the hotel lives who, seeing us in the taxi that first time we went to Nettlewood, waved to us till we were out of sight.

'Well, there – sad to say,' Bidfine went on, 'unruly children are now wont to hurl stones, so the taxi drivers aver, at their vehicles. You see, once their parents exerted control over them, but now they have picked up the bad habits of the Western world with its unbridled democracy!'

I wondered whether the taxi drivers hadn't picked up the Western world's habit of paranoia. It was also possible that their interdict on the Old Mountain was just one of those token anti-European gestures (with as much permanence as that taxi strike last time we were here) to show Islamic solidarity without endangering the financial favours of European governments. If so, the new Saudi residents appearing on the Mountain will scarcely notice it: visitors to Prince Faid's huge new 'development' (which I noticed going up) are unlikely to need a taxi to convey them, and therefore to appreciate the privilege that would be accorded them if they did. (A much greater sign of 'solidarity' is the intention of the Kuwaiti princess to knock down the grand old villa she has bought and replace it with a new one more to her taste: this exactly corresponds to the habit Moroccans have for centuries followed of simply moving on and rebuilding.)

Fatima now entered with the tea-tray, which included the kettle. This she removed and placed on top of the oil-stove. She then turned and went out of the room.

'Thank you, Fatima,' said Bidfine. As he got up to pour the tea, he showed again that stiffness of movement I'd observed as we entered the house, and he filled the cups from the right, even though the position we occupied made it easier to do so from the left. These things, I learned afterwards, G's medical eye had already noted and interpreted.

'No muffins, I'm afraid,' Bidfine apologised. 'The Spanish shop that did them – and the famous Porte's biscuits – is now Moroccan-owned, so that touch of civilisation has followed its many predecessors into oblivion.' He refilled the teapot from the kettle (no return visit from Fatima for the purpose) then placed it in the waste-paper basket. 'It won't go on bubbling and disturbing us there,' he explained. 'And later, when she collects the tea things, Fatima will take it back to the kitchen. We mustn't make her do another journey now she's all alone, poor thing.'

The revelations were coming thick and fast! Fatima alone? Where were Mustafa and all the rest of 'the family'?

'Mustafa,' said Bidfine when we enquired, 'is dead.'

(I may have imagined it but, for all his matter-of-fact tone, I was sure a shudder of emotion passed through him as he said this.)

'It is because Mustafa is dead,' he explained, 'that *Television* has come to Nettlewood, so that Fatima's brothers may have something to occupy them at night when they keep her company here as they must from motives of propriety as well as consolation, now that her – and my – poor Mustafa is no more. He was only forty – we think,' he went on, 'and she is barely twenty-five, married at fourteen or fifteen, but unlikely to repeat the experience, I'm afraid. Their lack of children will make potential husbands think she was barren. That is the way of things here.' He paused for a moment, then said: 'He was absolutely devoted to her. And to me. He always kept his eyes on the ground. Once in the garden he turned to me and said, "Master, you have soiled your hands." I don't want to seem patronising, but he was like a good dog. You know how one loves a dog?' (I nodded; I remembered Brigadier Hasta's remarks on the subject at the party.) 'Well, that's how I loved him.'

Of course, in saying this Bidfine was only describing the relationship as it had always been: one of old-fashioned master and servant. But inequality of that kind needn't exclude emotion and Bidfine was clearly very upset at Mustafa's death, and full of sympathy for his widow. Yet from a sense of breeding, or whatever snobbish concern he was allowing to dictate his behaviour, he spoke with mechanical precision and in a way that made him seem callous and unfeeling. His style would not allow him to show the emotion he genuinely felt, to admit his own vulnerability. He would go to any lengths, it seemed, to court the charge of heartlessness rather than run the risk of being thought sentimental: that celebrated English shying away from emotion and its hybrid expression, between tragedy and farce, that informs its life and literature. But as in literature style should never govern content, always the other way round; so in life ironic expression of emotion that is genuine is no more sincere than bald statement of emotion that isn't.

Meanwhile the sunset was a murky affair and soon over; cloud had succeeded the mist and been itself followed by rain. Darkness came with scarcely a hint that light had preceded it.

'It has a distinctly Nordic look tonight,' said Bidfine, switching on the lights. 'It's always different. That is the source of its never-ending appeal. That is why I shall remain here, come what may, living my life and entertaining charming guests like yourselves. If revolution comes, they will just have to come and get me, because I shall stay to the last, till the end, bitter or sweet as it may be. Unless of course,' he added, again with deceptive casualness, 'they take me away before then in an ambulance. As they did when I had my stroke – did I mention my stroke? Ah no! *You* mentioned Esmé St Clair's. Well, you see it's becoming the fashion!'

With this new revelation Bidfine was back on course for his irony: 'Well, having been invalided out of the army in 1940 – I fell off a mountain, they may have told you – I hadn't the length of service or whatever to qualify for the military hospital in Gib – though I am one of the few people here who can afford it! Those, like Brigadier Hasta, with the requisite military entrée, can't. So *nobody* uses it.'

This meant he was 'condemned', as he put it, to the Spanish hospital where Mustafa had died (after a heart attack). His grisly account of the place explained Esmé's reluctance to have anything to do with it. 'Those who enter seldom emerge,' said Bidfine. (Apparently it contains an individual nicknamed 'The Butcher' with a passion for amputation. 'I saw a patient with the simplest of wounds being asked as he fell under the anaesthetic to sign away his arm! Thankfully my frantic shakings of the head from behind deterred him from agreeing.')

'In my own case,' Bidfine explained, 'after the initial impact, I was – luckily for me – sufficiently compos mentis to have myself whisked out and away to the London Clinic – planes, wheelchairs and whatever laid on (England, I admit, still does one or two things well). Otherwise I can't imagine I should now, even with difficulty, be using my left arm to pour you drinks, for which I think it is time. All extremely tiresome and let us not dwell on it,' he went on, 'except to say that again it is fortunate you have your own transport, since driving is now a problem for me. I've had minor accidents – though not always of my own making. I assure you my own newly-acquired deficiencies are the least of it, when you know the general standard of driving here – not to mention walking. Last time I drove I had to stop violently for a pedestrian, and of course a boy on a bicycle – without lights – rammed me from behind. Naturally, when I sent for a policeman I got instead the boy's father demanding a hundred dirhams or it would cost me more in court. In fact, it cost *him* more in court because I could afford to take him there – again the value of money – and when he gave his lying evidence I said "May God forgive you!" in Arabic, at which the judge smiled and found in my favour.' Bidfine smiled himself. 'But it has rather put me off driving – not that I have much reason to go into town anyway. After all, I have wanted to cut myself off and that, in a word, is what I am now.' But, perhaps sensing delicate ground, he at once continued: 'I was of course besieged with offers of help from my relatives in England. A kind of group schadenfreude overtook them. They dreamt up all kinds of future catastrophes from which only their meddling intervention could save me. One offered to house-hunt on my behalf saying I was mad to live in these "uncivilised" countries and if I must have the sun why didn't I just winter in Gibraltar. Gibraltar! *Rarlly*, I ask you! If there's one thing worse than England it's an English colony. No! You may be sure I have taken care of that last loophole in my modus vivendi – born from sheer vanity at thitherto unfailing good health. In future I shall be lifted by helicopter from this very spot the moment the blow of fate falls. But at least that brief dicing with death confirmed my belief that the Greeks were right to condone slavery: they knew that incompetent people must be told what to do.'

This provided a cue for reiteration of his views on such

matters as 'post-war socialists knocking down Georgian "slums" and blaming the animal effects of the inhabitants on the buildings.' We had had this kind of thing before and on that occasion G had suggested perhaps if the buildings had been renovated sooner and better facilities installed they would not have become slums in the first place. Then, Bidfine had protested he was merely quoting the councils' views of the inhabitants. He said the same again now. We both laughed and said he was doing himself an injustice trying to appear a canting liberal when he was really such a magnificent reactionary. I told him I preferred him at his most crackpot to the prevailing view we're returning to in Britain (tomorrow!) that being proletarian is the same thing as being working-class; that being styleless, boorish and ill-mannered shows your heart is in the right place: with ordinary working people. (A terrible insult to ordinary, working people.)

I'm not sure Bidfine took my point because now he said: 'Here ordinary working people know their place. Here for that reason we can drink as we are doing out of these lovely glasses because my servants never chip or break anything.'

It was odd the way he kept referring to 'the servants' and 'their excellent qualities' in the plural. I had realised by now that only Fatima remained. Perhaps her husband's death had precipitated a general exodus. I looked at the picture on the wall of 'the family': there were four apart from Mustafa and Fatima. Where and why had they gone? Had their master's eccentric ways proved too much for them? I got no chance to pursue this – or even to think about it more myself – because when I turned to look at that photograph, pausing as I did so to read the title of a book that caught my eye, Bidfine said: 'Listen to me!' in a voice so imperative I could hardly believe the remark was being addressed to me. It sounded all the stranger for the usual urbane delivery that continued on either side of it, coming like a sudden alarming hiatus in an otherwise regular heartbeat.

I hardly had time to recover from this when something happened to add to the deranged atmosphere that had begun to develop: the lights went out. A darkness descended as total as I have known anywhere. Outside the heavy cloud cover allowed not even a glow in the night sky, far less moonlight, or even sight of the stars, and the lush vegetation gave the garden a blackness so deep it prevented the crudest shape or outline being visible.

Within, the room had taken on the feel of a tunnel, so impossible was it to make out even its walls or ceiling in the dark. Most eerie of all, the one object that, when my eyes had grown as accustomed as they ever would to the conditions, I could just distinguish was the silhouette of Bidfine's head, a thing made possible by the white stretches of his hair, sole source of luminosity remaining.

Bidfine of course – it seemed only natural – carried on as if nothing had happened. The smooth, cultivated voice continued on its measured way, as it probably would have done had this turned out to be the signal for the end of time. But it was just that composure I found most disturbing, that encouraged the mad idea which began to go through my mind. This was all part of a trap into which Bidfine had lured us. Desperate for some intelligent company, he intended to imprison us here.

I kept thinking of the character of Mr Todd in that grotesque episode – originally a short story – which Evelyn Waugh had later used as an alternative ending (publisher's demand) to his *Handful of Dust* (it was that book I had noticed as I turned to look at the wedding photograph). I had visions now of Bidfine asking us at any moment to begin reading *Bleak House* or something.

These fears were not allayed when suddenly Bidfine stopped speaking and another, graver, altogether more doom-laden voice could be heard coming from some distant corner of the room. Was this the guard summoned to arrange our confinement?

Then through the gloom I made out a small stretch of illuminated dial and realised Bidfine had switched on his battery-operated wireless (the Nettlewood word). 'A brief sortie into the outside world,' he said. 'Just in case the end has come.'

The voice was reading the news in the stentorian tone of a vanished age that only the World Service, museum-like, preserves. '...And if,' it was saying, 'the Russian fleet moves into the Gulf, the President states that he would have no choice but to see such action as an unequivocal and deliberate act of provocation...'

In the light – or rather darkness (two-fold) – of this, I began to wonder if it mattered so much what was going to happen to us. Nettlewood was probably as good a place as any to face the holocaust. Perhaps that was why Bidfine had come here.

But the radio was switched off as suddenly as it had been put on. 'As usual, nothing of importance,' said Bidfine.

A silence ensued which, for all the tension it generated, came as a respite after the sounds of the disembodied voices. But it was another voice, G's, that broke the tension, asking in the homely way of his slight Lancashire accent (more noticeable in the dark): 'Is this a natural event?'

'To those of us who live here,' Bidfine replied, in a tone so world-weary he could have been bidding a deathbed farewell, 'power failures are as natural as sand in the Sahara or fog on Lake Windermere. Besides, I find darkness a pleasant state. I find it conducive to reflection. But of course, when Mustafa was alive he would at once have brought me a candle.' He paused, and even in the dark I sensed a hesitation, a reluctance to go on, before he continued: 'Mustafa did everything that was wanted, was always ready at hand. And now he is gone. Dead of a heart attack and only forty years old.'

I began to find the darkness less sinister now than soothing and, like Bidfine, conducive to reflection. I thought of Baudelaire's dandy maintaining what he called 'the last resort of heroism in the midst of decadence'. The lines came back to me: 'Against the rising tide of triviality, and mediocrity, the dandy stands in brief revolt. He is superb, without warmth and full of melancholy, like the setting sun, the last representative of human pride drowning in a sea of democracy.'

In the cover of darkness Bidfine seemed more willing to unburden himself. 'My father died at almost the same age,' he said. 'When I was an infant. My mother and I left England as a result, travelled round in what is called genteel poverty. But it was poverty to us. It humiliated us, embittered us, frightened us. That's why I had to make money. Even so, my mother never got over his death. And now I don't suppose I shall ever get over Mustafa's. He was devoted to me. And I was to him. He loved me. I loved him. He died of a heart attack. And my heart was also affected.'

On the plane back (we came home a week ago – have simply carried on from where I left off) I sat next to a woman who'd known Bidfine in his Spanish days. She spoke of him in very warm terms; told me she'd been 'half in love with him'. He'd been especially kind to her during an 'emotional crisis', coming to see her regularly, always with presents and amusing stories that kept up her spirits. 'And of course,' she went on, 'he's devoted to that nephew of his. Which is why it's such a pity now he's married that his wife hates Morocco and just won't go there. So the boy doesn't either. It's terrible. And as for Tommy going to Gib...'

She left the sentence unfinished, but I needed no reminder of Bidfine's horror of the Rock. And I began to understand that peremptory 'Listen to me!' when I happened to glance at the wedding photograph on the wall.

A few days after getting back here I was stuck in a shop queue and, my thoughts at that moment on Nettlewood and its inhabitant, I found my eye caught by a packet on the shelf before me. It was labelled: Bidfine's Fondant Icing. Since then I have seen other products bearing the name. I have bought some of them. Bidfine's currants, Bidfine's raisins, Bidfine's dried fruit mixture. Yesterday I saw a poster:

Fine Bids from Bidfine's: BIDFINE – The Guarantee of Quality.

16 May

The east wind blows, the days are overcast. Spring has definitely arrived. Season not, alas, of renewal but ruthless extinction of the old and showy promotion of the new.

Sitting in the Nettlewood darkness, I formed impressions rather as I had that time at Fez. But whereas then it was parallels from Britain that shed light on Tangier, now it was the other way round. Now I saw the Tangieros as fag-end less of a Tangier society than a British one, and their plight as small-scale version of Britain's: going down not so much fighting as with the band playing and the show – the increasingly tawdry act of Being British – still going on. Today an ex-Prime Minister tells us we need 'a moral crusade' and the Archbishop of Canterbury insists 'the spirit of God is abroad' (winter-sunning himself, no doubt, while the nation freezes). But these are the dead leaves, still visible on the ground, under which though the earth is turning. People are coming here to live and work for whom the past means less than the chance of a prosperous present. And others who see no such prospect here are going abroad in a new kind of exile: formerly underpaid masters, now overpaid servants.

When I missed here the vitality of Tangier it was because I was looking for the old *imaginative* vitality I'd always known in Britain. Whereas really it is exactly the Tangier kind that exists here now: the same progress of life through decay and dereliction, recycling all in its path and turning it to new account, that I'd derived such exhilaration from on that first visit, while stumbling round the Phoenician ruins with Nina. Here, as in Tangier, that process is generating a cultural mix between the moribund of the old and the meretricious of the new, proceeding still against the rapidly fading backcloth of a Britain as dismantled and impossible to reassemble as the immaculate but no longer functioning contents of Harvey Lambert's house. We are all tradesmen now, all down there grubbing in the market place, plying our wares in our own kinds of medinas. And when we are not doing that we are visiting those outposts of the picturesque that are swiftly following our own into the museum. Renovation and conservation are the by-words here, and in Morocco the middle classes are moving back into the kasbahs that the Berbers are vacating. Following in our footsteps Morocco goes on struggling into the century that we are staggering out of.

★

Today I went into the offices of 'Morocco Bound'. I wanted to thank the Moroccan who runs it for his help. He was pleased to see me but asked why I hadn't turned up as promised on Tuesday.

'I did turn up on Tuesday, but you were closed.'

He looked puzzled. 'We don't close on Tuesdays.'

I said this Tuesday they were closed.

'Ah yes: this Tuesday we were closed. But normally we don't close on Tuesdays. Otherwise I would not have said to come in.'

As I was leaving, he asked: 'Have you been to Torquay?'

I said yes, but many years ago. It was very different now.

'Ah yes,' he said. 'It is very beautiful now. It is very new. In Morocco everything is old. Here you are wise. You knock down the old. Build the new.'

He said Torquay had a mild winter climate.

18 May

Particularly fine twilight here this evening.

From *Mediterranean Winter Resorts:*

Had it continued an English possession it is probable that Tangier would have become one of the favourite extra-European winter resorts for English people. But the barbarous character of the Government, the general insecurity of the country, combined with the mutual jealousies of the rival powers have effectually checked its development as a winter station, and prevented its fulfilling its natural destiny as a sanatorium for Europe.

Printed in the United Kingdom
by Lightning Source UK Ltd.
108121UKS00001B/225